SUBMARINES

JADE

Distributed by Omega Books Limited
1 West Street, Ware, Hertfordshire

Printed in Hong Kong

ISBN 0 907853 59 5

CONTENTS

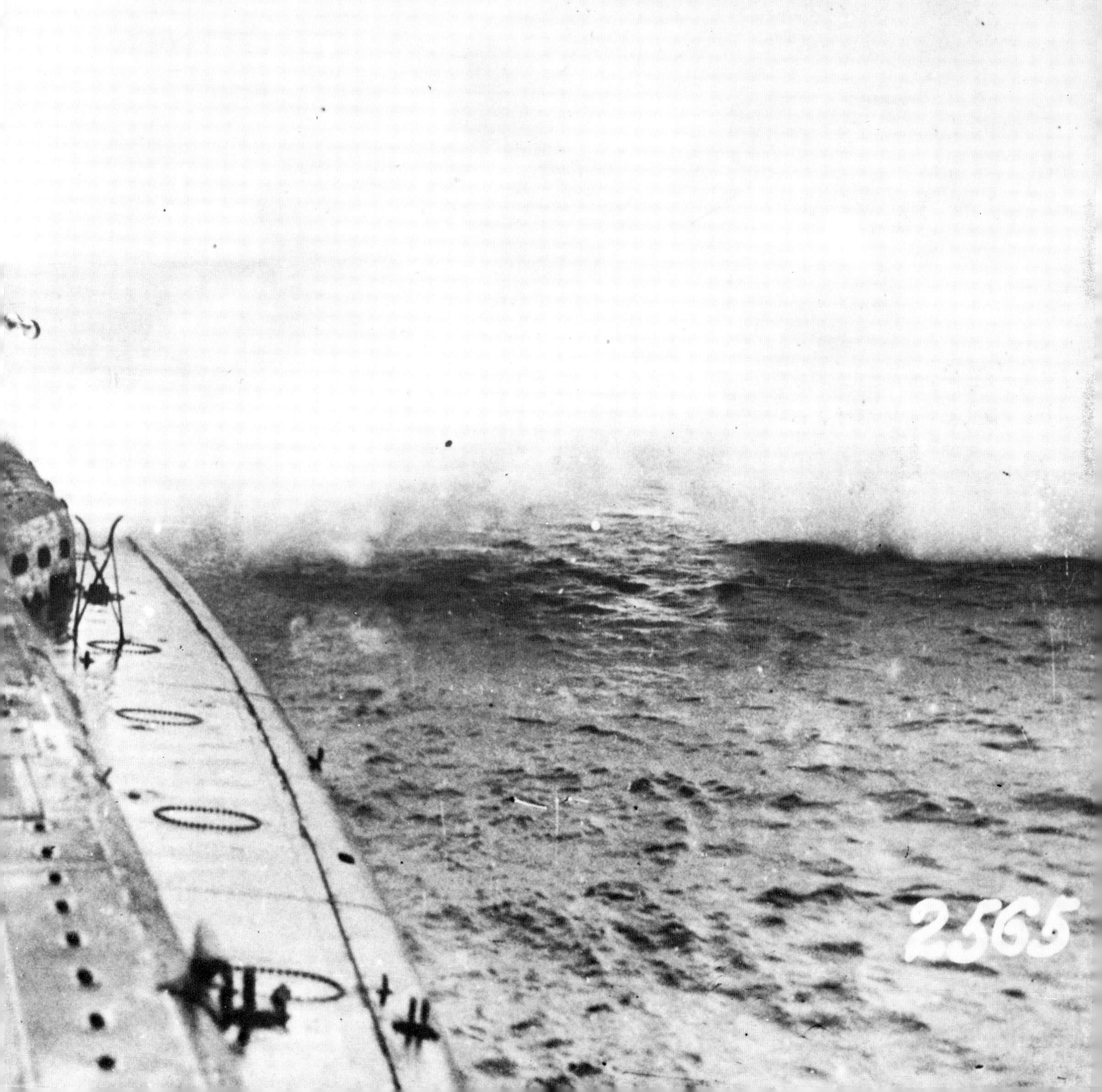

1914–1939

When World War I began in August 1914 the role of the submarine was obscured by a cloud of doubts, hopes and fears about what submarines *could* do and above all, what they *should* do. This applied to both of the two leading naval antagonists, Britain and Germany. For the previous ten years they had been obsessed with the race to build the strongest conventional fleet of battleships, and the British and Imperial German Navies had built submarines largely because everyone else had them. The British had taken to the submarine with all the more reluctance, because the submarine was seen as a sneaky underhand weapon to use against any honest surface fleet. As for the suggestion that enemy submarines might be used against merchant shipping, this would be such a barbaric violation of the rules of 'civilised' war that it was generally dismissed as unthinkable.

These rules, tentatively defined by the Hague Peace Conferences of 1899 and 1907, had laid it down that a warship wishing to sink an enemy merchant ship must first stop its victim, give clear warning of its intention, and afterwards provide for the safety of the castaway crew. Neutrals could be stopped and searched, and if found to be carrying war materials for a hostile power could be escorted to port and interned. But a few far-sighted men, headed in Britain by Admiral Lord Fisher, had by 1914 realised with growing apprehension that the submarine was a weapon to which such rules could not apply. The submarine, Fisher pointed out in a memorandom of January 1914, 'cannot capture the merchant ship; she has no spare hands to put a prize crew on board; little or nothing would be gained by disabling her engines or propeller; she cannot convey her into harbour; and, in fact, it is impossible for the submarine to deal with commerce in the light and provisions of accepted international law.' And he went on: 'There is nothing else the submarine can do except sink her capture . . . this submarine menace is a terrible one for British commerce and Great Britain alike, for no means can be suggested at present of meeting it except by reprisals.'

Prophetic words indeed, but they were regarded as fantastic by the British government and Admiralty alike and subsequently ignored. So far from deducing that submarines would, by reason of their very limitations, have no option but to sink their prey, the Admiralty had declared in a memorandum of December 1912 that the submarine had the smallest value of any vessel for attacks on trade. 'Therefore she will not affect the direct action in attack, which must be made by cruisers and other surface travelling vessels.'

This wishful thinking, that submarine attacks on merchant shipping would be considered *tabu*, was in total contrast to the conviction that warships were predestined targets for submarine attack. One of the commonest features on battleships, battle-cruisers and heavy cruisers down to 1914 was the distinctive diagonal barring of ships' sides with long booms, which could be swung out at right-angles to protect the ship with anti-torpedo nets when she lay at anchor. By 1914 the submarine was accepted, along with surface torpedo-boats and mines, as one of the three most insidious menaces to heavy surface warships. And the British, hag-ridden by the fear of having their numerical superiority in capital ships whittled away by German torpedoes and mines, were taking the submarine threat to their naval superiority very seriously indeed.

As far as the all-important North Sea theatre was concerned, British naval strategy in 1914 was the offspring of a weird marriage of confidence and fear. The confidence was that (for some reason best known to the German Admiralty) the outnumbered German High Seas Fleet would decide to come out and fight. The fear was that cumulative British losses from German mines and torpedoes would enable the High Seas Fleet eventually to fight a battle on even terms. Thus nothing would be gained by a close blockade of German ports—the British *wanted* the Germans to come out and fight. On the other hand it would be clearly suicidal for the British to court piecemeal destruction by the mine-and-torpedo menace. By 1912, therefore, unknown to the German Admiralty, the British had already decided against a close blockade of German ports in the event of war. Instead the massed battle squadrons of the British Grand Fleet would be held as far north as possible in Scottish waters, close enough to pounce on any sortie into the North Sea by the High Seas Fleet, but at extreme range from German submarine and torpedo attack. The huge natural anchorage of Scapa Flow in the Orkneys was finally chosen as the Grand Fleet's war base.

The Germans had no intention of throwing themselves into a sea war; they were gambling on a knockout victory on land, at the expense of the French and German Armies. German naval strategy was strictly opportunist. Warships already at sea were to make as big a nuisance of themselves on the high seas as possible, hopefully drawing off large numbers of British warships in pursuit. Lone British warships and isolated squadrons were to be lured to their doom in German coastal waters, either amid the dense minefields screening the German bases or under the guns of the High Seas Fleet in superior strength. But when the Grand Fleet stayed where it was in Scapa Flow, the embryo and untried U-boat force was sent out to attempt to carry the war into British waters.

At the outbreak of the war the German Navy only had 20 U-boats fit for service, and four of these (*U-1*, *U-2*, *U-3* and *U-4*) were suitable only for training. *U-5* to *U-18*, inclusive, were all powered by Körting heavy-oil engines which emitted sparks and dense clouds of white smoke when running on the surface; only three of the 18 bigger diesel-engined boats ordered in 1912–13 had been completed by August 1914, and the completion of the other 15 dragged on until October 1915. But on 6 August 1914, with the war barely 48 hours old, *Korvettenkapitän* Hermann Bauer led the first U-boat sortie into the North Sea. With ten U-boats (all of them heavy-oil boats) he planned to cruise to the Grand Fleet's front doorstep: a line from the Shetlands to Bergen in Norway.

This operation, the first joint war cruise by a flotilla of submarines, met with a funereal lack of success. Engine failure forced *U-9* to head back to base on 8 August. On the same day a British battle squadron was sighted off Fair Isle, midway between the Orkneys and Shetlands; *U-13* and *U-15* went in to attack, but the only torpedo fired missed the Dreadnought battleship *Monarch* and alerted the British force. Then *U-15*, separated from the rest of the flotilla, was surprised on the surface at dawn on the 9th by the light cruiser *Birmingham*. The British warship opened fire at once and increased speed to ram. As *Birmingham* came in for the kill her men heard hammering noises coming from inside *U-15*'s hull, suggesting that the U-boat had been crippled by main engine failure which her crew was trying to repair to the last. This was never confirmed because *Birmingham's* stem sliced *U-15* completely in two, the two halves of the U-boat going down with her entire complement of 29. And when, on the 12th, Bauer and the surviving U-boats returned to Heligoland, they heard that a second of their number had been lost. This was *U-13*, which had strayed into a German minefield and been sunk quickly and quietly on 9 August.

German World War I painting of the scene in a U-boat's control room.

A second U-boat sweep had been sent out on 8 August, while Bauer and his men were still at sea. This was prompted by extraordinarily inaccurate German intelligence, which had surmised that the British Expeditionary Force was already at sea and heading for a landfall in Belgium. (In fact the BEF did not sail until a week later, and when it did it disembarked in France.) Four of the new diesel-engined U-boats sailed to intercept the non-existent British transports. The diesel boats had been rushed into service; 'teething troubles' were naturally rife, and three of them turned back with mechanical defects. Only *Kapitänleutnant* Otto Hersing in *U-21* reached the patrol area, to return empty-handed.

These first cruises, however, were of immense value. They gave German submariners their first vital operational experience, and located mechanical and design weaknesses which could be tackled and either overcome or omitted from new boats. Apart from this the first U-boat sorties, so far to the north, not only confirmed the 'submarine neurosis' of the British Grand Fleet but raised it to ever higher levels. False economy in the last two years of peace had left Scapa Flow—unlike the German North Sea bases—without any artificial defences capable of keeping out enemy submarines. There were no booms, no lines of blockships, no shore searchlights, no belts of mines sealing the channels between the islands of Orkney ringing the Flow. Nor had any weapons been developed capable of attacking a submerged submarine. 'Anti-submarine picket-boats' nervously patrolled the Flow, preposterously armed with large bags and hammers: the bag was for

Admiral Sir John Jellicoe, according to Churchill, was 'the only man who could have lost the war in an afternoon'. Jellicoe commanded the world's mightiest battle fleet—and found his tactical movements paralysed by fears of the German submarine menace.

ramming over a conveniently presented periscope, the hammer for smashing the periscope lens.

As a result any freak ripple, any lone seal putting its head up was likely to be reported as a periscope, sending the world's mightiest battle fleet stampeding out to sea and safety. It happened for the first time on 1 September 1914 and Admiral Sir John Jellicoe kept the Grand Fleet at sea for four days before he deemed it safe to return. Even then he only sent the 3rd Battle Squadron back to Scapa, taking the bulk of the Fleet to Loch Ewe on the west coast of Scotland. While the panic was at its height, Otto Hersing came probing into the Firth of Forth in *U-21*. He was spotted and chased out to sea, but on the afternoon of the 5th, off St Abb's Head, *U-21* fell in with the British light cruiser *Pathfinder* and her destroyer flotilla. In seas so rough that the British could not at first believe that a torpedo attack had been made, Hersing fired a single torpedo which sent the little cruiser to the bottom with the loss of 259 of her complement of 296. The U-boat arm had claimed its first victim.

The withdrawal of the Grand Fleet to the west coast of Scotland because of the U-boat panic must be counted one of the greatest missed opportunities of World War I. If the German naval Zeppelins had discovered that the Grand Fleet was neither in the North Sea nor in Scapa, there would have been nothing to prevent the full strength of the High Seas Fleet from sweeping into the English Channel, severing the BEF's communications with home on the eve of the Battle of the Marne.

Within three weeks of Hersing's kill off St Abb's Head the U-boat arm struck again—and this time resoundingly. On 22 September 1914 *Kapitänleutnant* Otto Weddigen, in *U-9*, became the only submarine captain in naval history to sink three enemy cruisers in a single hour. The ships in question were the old *Cressy* class cruisers *Aboukir*, *Hogue* and *Cressy* (completed in 1901–02) and on the morning of the 22nd they were parading up and down the southeastern stretch of the North Sea known as the 'Broad Fourteens'. There was no compelling reason for maintaining this exposed beat, perilously close to German waters—other than the damning comment of the Admiralty Chief of Staff that 'We've *always* maintained a squadron on the Broad Fourteens'. But nor was there any compelling reason to order their withdrawal, and the Admiralty neglected to do so. The cruisers were screened by two destroyer flotillas from Harwich, but these were forced back to base by bad weather on the 17th, leaving the ageing trio on its own; and the cruisers were still patrolling the 'Broad Fourteens' when Weddigen found them on the morning of 22 September.

A stiff wind was kicking up five-foot 'white-caps' on the sea and the British lookouts had failed to spot *U-9*'s periscope when Weddigen fired his first bow torpedo at *Aboukir* at 6.30 am. He fired submerged at a depth of about 12 feet, allowing his torpedo a straight run without being deflected by the wave crests, and scored a direct hit. Captain Drummond of the *Aboukir* believed that he had hit a mine, and made the fatal error of ordering *Hogue* and *Cressy* to close and assist. They stopped and lowered boats, presenting Weddigen with two perfectly positioned, stationary targets. He could not miss, and at 7.30 am *Cressy* followed *Hogue* and *Aboukir* to the bottom. Weddigen had made excellent use of the tumbling seas as camouflage, never showing enough periscope to give the British a solitary clue to their tormentor's whereabouts. The Harwich destroyers had sailed to rejoin the cruisers early the same morning; they finally came pounding up to the scene of the disaster, but not in time to prevent the loss of 1459 officers and men out of 2200. The destroyers tried to intercept Weddigen as he withdrew to a hero's welcome in Germany, but he evaded them with ease.

With the war not seven weeks old, the 'damned unEnglish' weapon had inflicted one of the most humiliating and one-sided defeats in the history of the Royal Navy. '*More men lost than by Lord Nelson in all his battles put together!*' raged Lord Fisher. Weddigen's feat did nothing for the morale of the Grand Fleet. 'I *long* for a submarine defence at Scapa; it would give me such a feeling of confidence. I can't sleep half so well inside as when outside, mainly because I feel we are risking such a mass of valuable ships in a place where, if a submarine did get in, she practically has the British Dreadnought Fleet at her mercy.' Those were not the words of an apprehensive midshipman but of the Grand Fleet C-in-C, Admiral Jellicoe, writing to First Lord Winston Churchill on 30 September. And the U-boat arm continued to give substance to Jellicoe's fears. On 15 October Weddigen and *U-9* struck again, this time at the Northern Patrol of old cruisers enforcing the blockade of Germany between Scotland and Norway. East of Aberdeen, Weddigen stalked three *Edgar* class cruisers which frustrated him for hours

Captain Johnson stands forlornly atop the capsized hull of his cruiser *Cressy*, torpedoed with *Hogue* and *Aboukir* on 22 September 1914. This was the only occasion in naval history when a submarine sank three enemy cruisers in a single hour.

with repeated changes of course and speed—one of the earliest and most efficacious anti-submarine measures adopted by the British. Then, suddenly, *Hawke* dropped her guard and hove-to in order to pick up mail from her consort *Endymion*. As on the 'Broad Fourteens' three weeks before, Weddigen snatched the opportunity. He fired a single torpedo which sank *Hawke* with the loss of 500 lives, virtually her entire complement.

Twenty-four hours after *Hawke* went down, the humiliation of 1 September was repeated in Scapa Flow. This time there were several 'periscope sightings' and one reported 'torpedo track' in the Flow. Out of its anchorage fled the Grand Fleet, not to return until 9 November. Jellicoe withdrew the Fleet to Lough Swilly in Northern Ireland—over 300 miles from where it would have been of any use if the High Seas Fleet had chosen to come out. 'We are hunted about the sea', lamented Commander Drax in the *Lion*, flagship of the battle-cruiser squadron, 'and have nowhere we can rest.' But the Grand Fleet's sense of nakedness began slowly to abate after its return to Scapa. Work on the base defences was now well advanced and on the 23rd *U-18*, attempting to creep into Scapa Flow, was intercepted in Hoxa Sound by a trawler. Damaged by gunfire, *U-18* crawled out into the Pentland Firth but was forced to scuttle herself—a heartening reminder that the U-boats were not invulnerable. Month by month the defences were improved, and by 1915 the Grand Fleet was at last able to feel secure in its anchorage.

What remained, however, was the British fear of being lured within range of German submarines. This was shown during the Battle of the Dogger Bank (24 January 1915) when Admiral Beatty's battle-cruisers intercepted a weaker German battle-cruiser force under Admiral Hipper, and gave chase. At the height of the action, Beatty reported, 'submarines were reported on the starboard bow and I personally observed the wash of a torpedo two points on our starboard bow'. Beatty's instinctive reaction to this non-existent threat—there was not a U-boat within 60 miles—was to order his ships to swing sharply away to port, and Hipper's battle-cruisers escaped. The British had been granted the boon for which they had yearned since the outbreak of war—a fair crack at the High Seas Fleet, or even part of it—but their submarine neurosis had made them drop the catch.

Opposite: Artist's impression of the British submarine *B11* lounging on the surface after torpedoing the Turkish battleship *Messudieh* in the Dardanelles (13 December 1914). Actually, Lieutenant Holbrook torpedoed his victim after closing submerged to a range of 80 yards; he then watched her sink through his periscope. But this was only the prelude to *B11*'s epic retreat through the Dardanelles minefields—blind, due to instrument failure—which set a new record of nine hours submerged, remarkable for so small a boat.

By the time of the Dogger Bank action the potentialities of the submarine had already been demonstrated in the Mediterranean—this time by the British. Turkey had entered the war on the side of Germany and Austria-Hungary at the beginning of November. This added the blockade of Turkey to the task of keeping the Austro-Hungarian fleet safely bottled up in the Adriatic Sea. The most obvious point at which the French and British might exploit their superiority at sea and carry the war to the Turks was the Dardanelles. This narrow and crooked strait led directly to Constantinople and offered the chance of an Anglo-French link-up with the Russians in the Black Sea. Unfortunately this was just as obvious to the Turks and their German advisers. The Dardanelles were known to be densely mined and covered from either shore by emplaced guns. No conventional surface fleet could live in the Dardanelles and prospects of lone submarines running under the defences were highly questionable. But the British were the first to give it a try.

In late 1914 the only British submarines in the eastern Mediterranean were three small boats of the 'B' class. These were petrol-engined, of doubtful submerged endurance and lacking a gun with which to fight if forced to the surface. But on 13 December 1914 Lieutenant Norman Holbrook entered the mouth of the Dardanelles in *B11*. Despite the strong currents in the strait Holbrook managed to work *B11* past the lower minefields and approach Çanakkale (Chanak), the narrowest defile below the Sea of Marmara. Below Çanakkale he found the old Turkish battleship *Messudieh*, approached submerged to the point-blank range of 80 yards, and sank her. But on turning for home Holbrook ran into severe trouble. As on most early British submarines, *B11*'s compass was mounted outside the hull to prevent it from being affected by the submarine's residual magnetism; the compass card was viewed by the helmsman through lenses. But now these lenses became fogged with condensation. With no compass readings to steer by, Holbrook had no choice but to navigate by dead reckoning, guessing at his whereabouts by taking hasty surveys through the periscope. During her hazardous retreat, much of it spent bumping along the bottom, *B11* spent over nine hours submerged—a feat beyond all expectations for a boat of her size. When *B11* finally rejoined the fleet her battery was completely exhausted. For this fine achievement Holbrook got the VC, his first Lieutenant the DSO, and every man in the crew received the DSC or the DSM, according to his rank. Hersing and Weddigen were the first submarine captains to sink enemy warships in the open sea, but Holbrook was the first to sink an enemy warship in waters theoretically safe from attack.

The year 1915 opened with another humiliation for the British in home waters, dispelling the fond belief still lingering in some quarters that the English Channel was somehow immune from penetration by U-boats. At 2.30 am on 1 January the pre-Dreadnought battleship *Formidable* was torpedoed and sunk by *U-24* off Start Point in the western Channel. This latest sinking came about largely because several British admirals, even after the painful lessons of the past few months, still considered the submarine to be an overrated weapon. (A similar phenomenon cropped up 25 years later at the outset of World War II, when some admirals obstinately held to the belief that a warship's guns automatically spelled defeat for air attacks. This myth was not finally dispelled until Japanese aircraft sunk the *Repulse* and *Prince of Wales* in December 1941.) One such diehard admiral at the end of 1914 was Sir Lewis Bayly, commanding the Channel Fleet. *Formidable* was lost when, as the rearmost ship in a squadron proceeding in neat line-ahead, she was steaming placidly along a dead straight course in bright moonlight at a leisurely ten knots, making no evasive movements whatsoever. For his serene complacency in neglecting even the most rudimentary anti-submarine precautions, Bayly was sacked from command of the Channel Fleet. It was a timely example, doubling as the Admiralty's official announcement that the old methods of waging war at sea could no longer be accepted as adequate.

There was just as much reluctance to accept this fact in Germany as there was in Britain. The German decision to wage submarine commerce warfare against Britain, taken in February 1915, was not a sudden, ruthless move by the German government. It had grown uncertainly from the unforeseen circumstances created by six months of a war which, so far from ending by Christmas, had produced an entrenched stalemate with no immediate solution in sight. As the German Armies in France and Belgium dug in to defend their gains, the role of the German Navy was automatically enhanced. The U-boat arm was clearly the only force capable of inflicting real damage on Britain's fleets—mercantile as well as naval.

Most of the German surface warships at large on the high seas in August 1914 had been rounded

up and sunk by January 1915, and the few survivors still eluding the Allied squadrons were living on borrowed time. Thus, by default, the task of attacking Britain's vital imports of war materials was bound to pass to the U-boats sooner or later. Between August 1914 and February 1915 their achievements against British commerce remained slight: only ten British merchantmen sunk since 13 October 1914, when *U-17* had stopped, searched and sunk the steamship *Glitra* off the Norwegian coast (following the provisions of International Law). But this insignificant performance by the U-boats was the result of the restrictions imposed on the submarine's *modus operandi* by the Hague Convention. If the U-boats could be allowed to attack merchantmen without warning, vastly different results could be achieved.

The most dramatic implication of unrestricted submarine warfare was its extension to merchantmen flying neutral flags as well as those flying the Red Ensign. To this Germany was able to retort that the Royal Navy's wartime insistence on its traditional 'right of search' of all vessels was itself a violation of International Law. Moreover, the wearing of neutral flags as a defensive measure was an age-old *ruse de guerre*. If the British continued to use neutral shipping to carry their war imports, and to advise their merchant skippers to fly neutral flags, Germany could hardly be expected to tolerate such a one-sided state of affairs.

The risk of a 'massacre of the innocents' among civilian women and children if passenger liners were attacked was another objection which the Germans were able to parry. The British themselves had involved passenger liners in the naval war by requisitioning such vessels as auxiliary merchant cruisers on the outbreak of war. Liners were also able to be used as troop carriers as well as to carry large quantities of war materials. No warship—surface vessel or submarine—could be expected to pass up such a target, and if civilians persisted in sailing in liners after due warning had been given they would have only themselves to blame.

Such, in outline, was the reasoning behind the first German attempt at a deliberate submarine campaign against British commerce, which duly opened on 18 February 1915 after the fortnight's warning had elapsed. It was certainly not an unrestricted campaign: ships flying neutral flags still had to be positively identified as hostile or in breach of the neutrality laws before they could be attacked. Nor were there anything like *enough* U-boats (only 22 in mid-

Oil bleeds into the sea as a merchantman sinks by the stern after a U-boat attack.

Above: Death of the *Lusitania*, the nightmare come true.
Right: American headlines above the bare-faced German statement that *Lusitania* 'was naturally armed with guns'.

February) to carry out an effective campaign. The time—four days—taken up in sailing out round the British Isles to reach a patrol area on Britain's Western Approaches, plus the time needed for repairs, maintenance and replenishment with stores and ammunition between patrols, meant that on average only four U-boats could stay on patrol at a time. For all that, the U-boats managed to sink 39 British merchantmen from 18 February to the end of April, during which period only four U-boats were lost.

The foremost casualty was Germany's first U-boat ace, Otto Weddigen, lost with his crew when *U-29* was sunk on 18 March. Weddigen, patrolling off the Moray Firth, caught a British battle squadron exercising at sea and attacked. But his opening torpedo missed the battleship

Neptune and an alert lookout spotted *U-29*'s periscope from *Dreadnought*. Beautifully handled, *Dreadnought* wheeled out of line, steered for the periscope's 'feather' of white water and trampled the U-boat under before Weddigen had had the chance to go deep. On his previous patrol Weddigen, who favoured surface attacks against merchantmen, had sunk six merchant ships in a single patrol and earned the nickname of the 'polite pirate' from the British. His death beneath the keel of an 18,000-ton battleship was not likely to encourage other U-boat captains to take liberties with 32,000-ton oceanliners.

The most notorious event of the new U-boat campaign was, of course, the sinking of the liner *Lusitania* in the early afternoon of 7 May, with the loss of 1201 men, women and children and a contingent of 128 American citizens. The culprit was *Kapitänleutnant* Walter Schwieger of *U-20*. On his last patrol in the North Sea, he had nursed his leaking U-boat home after having narrowly survived a ramming attack by a merchantman he had challenged on the surface. He saw no reason to spare *Lusitania*, which he knew to have been correctly warned of the existence of the German 'war zone' around Britain, and which he believed to be a potential troop-carrier and natural vehicle for war contraband. Stubborn official secrecy, extending to the British Admiralty and the White House in Washington, means that the precise nature of *Lusitania*'s cargo will probably never be known. But a large explosion—and not exploding

THE WEATHER.

Fair and somewhat cooler Sunday; Monday, fair; moderate southwest to west winds.

New York American

THE TWENTIETH CENTURY NEWSPAPER

This Edition of THE AMERICAN consists of the following Sections:

No. 11,617. Copyright, 1915, by Star Company — SUNDAY — NEW YORK, MAY 9, 1915 — SUNDAY — Registered in U. S. Patent Office. — PRICE FIVE CENTS

LUSITANIA DEAD 1,256---115 AMERICANS GERMANY OFFICIALLY ADMITS SINKING SHIP

U. S. WILL ACT QUICKLY; DRASTIC STEPS URGED AS INDIGNATION RISES

Wilson Besieged with Telegrams and Situation Is Regarded as Most Momentous in Many Years—Gerard Cabled for Germany's Explanation

Washington, May 8.—The rising tide of popular indignation against the sinking of the Lusitania by a German submarine with the consequent enormous loss of life of American citizens has caused Administration officials to indicate more positive views for comprehensive action than was revealed by those officials earlier

HUNDREDS MASSED ON DECK AS LINER REARED IN HER DEATH PLUNGE

Survivors Tell Thrilling Stories of Last Fateful Moments—Sixty Perish as Lifeboat Falls—Mothers Clasping Dead Babies Picked Up in Water

Special Cable to International News Service.

Queenstown, May 8.—Thrilling stories of the Lusitania disaster were told by survivors who landed here. F. J. Gauntlett, of New York, traveling in company with A. L. Hopkins, president of the Newport News Shipbuilding Co. (who is missing),

GERMANY'S OFFICIAL STATEMENT

Berlin, Via Wireless to London, May 9, 2:45 A. M.

THE following official communication was issued to-night:

"The Cunard liner Lusitania was yesterday torpedoed by a German submarine and sank.

"The Lusitania was naturally armed with guns, as were recently most of the English mercantile steamers. Moreover, as is well known here, she had large quantities of war material in her cargo.

"Her owners, therefore, knew to what danger the passengers were exposed. They alone bear all the responsibility for what has happened.

"Germany, on her part, left nothing undone to repeatedly and strongly warn them. The Imperial Ambassador in Washington even went so far as to make a public warning, so as to draw attention to this danger. The English

FROHMAN'S BODY IS FOUND; VANDERBILT AND HUBBARD LOST

London, May 8.—The first list of identified dead in the Lusitania disaster was given out here this afternoon. The bodies of the following persons have been recovered and positively identified, and are being embalmed:

DR. F. S. PEARSON, of New York.
MRS. AMELIA McDONALD.
PATRICK CALLON.
ARTHUR FOLEY.

Propaganda in denial of the heated atrocity stories: men of a German U-boat prepare to help castaways in their lifeboats. The giving of the survivors' position and recommended course to the nearest landfall became commonplace.

boilers—blew open her forward hull and took her to the bottom in 18 minutes. This can hardly be attributed to the destructive effect of *U-20*'s torpedoes. Only the previous day Schwieger had torpedoed two Harrison Line steamers, *Candidate* and *Centurion*. *Candidate* only sank after two hours when Schwieger perforated her hull at the waterline with shellfire; *Centurion* suffered two torpedoes and still took 80 minutes to sink.

With *Lusitania* the tragic loss of life was boosted by the ship's rapid list, confusion among the passengers and safety provisions which would be considered grossly inadequate by modern standards. Allied propaganda had a field day with the 'massacre' of women and children, omitting any sustained comment on the fact that the victims' menfolk had deliberately taken a dangerous risk. There was even less eagerness to admit that the British Admiralty had not exactly exerted itself in providing an escort through the war zone for *Lusitania*. Over 48 hours before *Lusitania* was hit, the Admiralty had known that U-boats were operating off southern Ireland. But the light cruiser *Juno*, originally detailed to rendezvous with *Lusitania* west of Fastnet, had been ordered back to Queenstown because of her 'unsuitability' to meet submarine attack—without Captain Turner of the *Lusitania* being told. Had *Lusitania* come within Schwieger's periscope view with *Juno* in attendance it would probably have been a different story. *Lusitania* was far too big a ship to be zig-zagged at 20 knots—certainly not with fare-paying passengers on board, whose custom the Cunard Company hoped to keep.

Though the *Lusitania* incident did not bring the United States into the war, repeated German sinkings of ships carrying American citizens continued to incense American public opinion and worry the Kaiser's statesmen. After *U-24* sank the British steamer *Arabic* on 19 August, killing three Americans, Washington's protest was so sharp that diplomatic caution prevailed in Germany. A new order went out on 30 August: passenger steamers were no longer to be attacked by submerged submarines, or without warning having been given and passengers and crew safely taken off. With the U-boats thus obliged once more to expose themselves on the surface, the inevitable result was the suspension of the campaign. Three weeks later, on 18 September, all U-boats were ordered to be withdrawn from the English Channel and Western Approaches.

All in all, the first German submarine campaign of February-September 1915 deserves to rank with Bonaparte's Italian campaign of 1796–97, or the debut of Guderian's Panzers in the Polish campaign of September 1939, as one of the most prominent milestones in the history of modern warfare. It saw the submarine come of age as the first modern weapon to make war a universal scourge, rather than a professional duel between rival armies and fleets. In the short term nothing decisive was accomplished: the British built more merchant ships than they lost, and the Germans built more U-boats than *they* lost. But in the long term the first U-boat offensive was, beyond question, a completely successful experiment. In 1915 U-boats destroyed 748,000 tons of British merchant shipping, a monthly average of over 62,333 tons and an increase of over a hundredfold on the meagre 600 tons sunk per month between August and December 1914. Given all the restrictions under which the U-boats had to operate in 1915, this was an unanswerable demonstration of the potential of the submarine and the efficacy of undersea commerce war. By January 1916 Admiral von Holtzendorff, Chief of the German Naval Staff, was able to inform Chancellor Bethmann Hollweg that 'If after the winter season, that is to say under suitable weather conditions, the economic war by submarines be begun again with every means available and without restrictions which from the outset must cripple its effectiveness, a defi-

nite prospect may be held out that, judged by previous experience, British resistance will be broken in six months at the outside.'

In 1915 the U-boat arm had gained all the salient knowledge to allow such a confident prediction to be made. Perhaps the most important lesson was the immense value of a deck gun which, when fired at a victim's waterline, was a far more economical way of sinking ships than the costly torpedo. Gun ammunition also took up less stowage space than torpedoes (only eight of which could be carried) and allowed U-boats to stay longer on patrol. The Germans also used the 1915 campaign to diversify the U-boat arm and try out their small coastal U-boats, the 'UB' class, originally armed only with two bow torpedo tubes. These boats were small enough to be shipped in sections by rail and assembled at the Austrian port of Pola, to operate against the Allies in the Adriatic. Also introduced in 1915 was the 'UC' class of mine-laying submarine, the first 15 boats armed with nothing heavier than a machine gun and carrying 12 mines in six vertical launching-tubes. (German mines accounted for 77,000 tons of British shipping in 1915.) The 'UB' and 'UC' boats made up the Flanders Flotilla based at Bruges close to the British coastal shipping lanes; it was formed on 29 March. In August 1915, the most effective month of the campaign, the Germans had 13 boats of all classes at sea and pushed British merchant shipping losses up to a record 148,400 tons.

The factor which proved of greatest assistance to the Germans in their first U-boat campaign was the complete failure of the British to develop

'We live again'—fanciful depiction of German submariners cheering as the periscope of a hunting British submarine passes close alongside. Such episodes were inevitable until submarines were fitted with sound-detecting hydrophones.

anti-submarine weapons and tactics. Lacking the means to detect submerged submarines, they nevertheless tried to take the offensive against the U-boats without realising that they were relying on the enemy making mistakes—never the safest of assumptions in war. The British tried to seal off the Dover Straits with a vast barrage of anti-submarine minefields and nets, the idea being that a snagged U-boat would trigger an indicator buoy, reveal its presence and be smashed as it lay helpless. For U-boats which escaped the British mines, the explosive sweep—a charge towed beneath the surface—was brought into service at the end of 1914, but the nets could be by-passed via their gaps, dived under or pierced; the minefields were a joke. British mines tended either not to explode when hit, or to drift from their laid positions. Only three U-boats (*U-5*, *U-11* and *U-37*) were sunk by mines in the Dover Straits and English Channel between August 1914 and December 1915. The explosive sweep was a marginally better idea, but was only of any use when a U-boat or periscope was actually sighted and the surface patrols given some idea of their quarry's course. *U-8*, sunk on 4 March 1915, was the only boat sunk by explosive sweeps in the Dover Straits in 1915.

The decoy or 'Q-ship', an innocent-looking vessel armed with concealed guns for the discomfiture of U-boats attacking on the surface, was a typical British half-measure in 1915. Q-ships accounted for three U-boats towards the end of the campaign—*U-36* in July, *U-27* in August, *U-41* in September—but once the

Demonstration of hydrophone positioning from a flying-boat's cockpit.

C R Fleming-Williams' painting of flying-boats attacking a U-boat, crippled and unable to dive.

Germans learned of their employment U-boat captains naturally tended to be wary. Indeed, so far from countering the U-boat menace, Q-ships helped increase it by strengthening the German case for a completely unrestricted offensive. Down to the end of the war Q-ships sank or helped sink 14 U-boats—but 31 Q-ships were lost in the process, torpedoed by U-boat skippers determined to take no chances. Another more cumbersome and elaborate half-measure was a British decoy towing a submerged submarine, communicating with the latter by telephone. Once a U-boat was sighted the British submarine would slip its tow and ambush the U-boat. Using this method the British submarine *C24* managed to sink *U-40* off Aberdeen in June 1915; but as with the Q-ship tactic, the danger of towed British submarines only encouraged U-boats to torpedo likely-looking fishing boats, especially if they seemed to be towing something.

But the real problem, perfectly summed up by Arthur J Marder in *From the Dreadnought to Scapa Flow*, was the British Admiralty's failure to diagnose the threat correctly:

'There was, at the Admiralty and afloat, altogether too much talk about "offensive action" against U-boats and far too little thought given to what was meant by "offensive action". What was, in effect, meant was trying to mine and bomb the U-boats in their bases, and, above all, to hunt them to destruction at sea. None of these measures was successful. The dogma "Seek out and destroy the enemy" governed all activities and precluded rational action. While the main difficulty with hunting tactics at this time was the lack of efficient submarine detectors of submerged submarines, the strategy of hunting was fundamentally unsound; it left the initiative to the elusive enemy. As a consequence, hunting became a succession of futile follow-up operations after U-boats had achieved successful attacks in a diversity of places. . . . The so-called hunting of submarines was a waste of effort and of resources except very infrequently when luck intervened and a U-boat captain made a mess of things. Indicator nets used in narrow waters were an attempt to overcome the problem of under-water detection of submarines, but they had severe limitations and were often disappointing.

'In the event, it was "defensive measures" such as the arming and routing of merchantmen which proved much more successful in curbing the U-boats' successes, but what, eventually and decisively, defeated them was the so-called 'defensive' measure of convoy. This was because it concentrated the main anti-submarine effort where it was most likely to be effectual.'

The British failure to assign top-priority status to the U-boat menace in early 1915 is partly explained by the fact that the campaign opened as the Allies were preparing for their own assault on the Dardanelles, first with warships alone (February/March) and then with large-scale troop landings on the Gallipoli peninsula (April). The strategic implications of the Dardanelles venture were not missed by the Germans; nor was the ensuing concentration of Allied naval units and shipping in the eastern Mediterranean, which in 1915 became the target for a parallel U-boat offensive.

Germany had already pledged U-boat reinforcements for her ally Austria, in the form of 'UB' class boats sent overland in sections to Pola. *UB-1* and *UB-15* eventually joined the Austrian Navy as *U-10* and *U-11*, and five more of the first 17 'UB' boats completed in 1915 went to Pola. But the German Admiralty also decided to send the big seagoing U-boats into the Mediterranean to help the Turks hold Gallipoli.

On 25 April, the day of the British landings on Gallipoli, Otto Hersing sailed from Germany in *U-21*, and after refuelling and repairing at Pola arrived off Gallipoli on 25 May. There he found targets galore. The British warships swarming off the beaches, trying to give fire support to the wretched troops ashore, had heard that U-boats were on their way out to the Mediterranean and were already gripped by the same U-boat neurosis which had swept the Grand Fleet in the first months of the war. But apart from the deployment of anti-torpedo nets on the ships and much aimless steaming to and fro, there were if anything even less effective anti-submarine measures than in home waters. Hersing had bad luck with his first three torpedoes, which missed the Russian cruiser *Askold* and the British battleships *Swiftsure* and *Vengeance*. He then spent two hours stalking the battleship *Triumph*, chose his moment well and sent her to the bottom with a single torpedo.

Though *U-21*'s periscope was sighted by the aghast onlookers ashore, Hersing evaded his disorganised naval pursuers and lay on the bottom for 28 hours until forced to surface and

British submarine *E14* bound for the Dardanelles, leaves Mudros with Commander Boyle (in overcoat) on the bridge.

recharge batteries by night. On the 27th he sighted the battleship *Majestic* with her torpedo nets out and a host of small patrol boats in attendance. Once again Hersing waited for an unimpeded shot, then fired a single torpedo which went clean through *Majestic*'s net and sank her. The result of this second sinking was momentous: all Allied capital ships were promptly withdrawn to the island of Lemnos, depriving the troops on Gallipoli of heavy-calibre fire support from the sea. Even if, by some miracle, the troops had broken through the Turkish defences on Gallipoli, the U-boat fear implanted by Hersing's arrival would have prevented the Allied fleet from lying close enough to the Dardanelles to cover the clearing of the Turkish minefields inside, then advancing in support of the land forces.

Following the exploit of *B11* back in December 1914, British submarines spearheaded the assault on the Dardanelles by forcing the straits submerged and emerging into the Sea of Marmara. The Australian Navy was the first to make it, when Lieutenant-Commander H D Stoker and *AE2* broke through into the Marmara on 26 April having sunk a Turkish gunboat *en route*. He was followed within 48 hours by Lieutenant-Commander E C Boyle in *E14*. *AE2* fell victim to a Turkish torpedo-boat on 29 April but Boyle ran amok with his tor-

Top: The crew of HMS *Grampus* cheer *E11* (Nasmith) as she emerges from the Dardanelles. Above: Master weapon in the Marmara, essential for 'all-round' raiding—the gun of submarine *E2*.

pedoes, destroying Turkish troop and ammunition transports. *E14* lingered in the Marmara for a week after her last torpedo had been fired, preventing any Turkish transports from crossing to Gallipoli by the mere threat of her presence.

The third British boat to penetrate the Marmara was *E11* (Lieutenant-Commander M E Dunbar Nasmith), who set out on her mission on 18 May. Nasmith's exploits on this cruise made him a legend in the British submarine service. Once in the Marmara he started by capturing a small *dhow* which he used as mobile camouflage, lashing *E11* alongside, trimmed down and virtually invisible. After sinking a gunboat and a transport loaded with guns, gun mountings and ammunition, Nasmith chased a third transport into the port of Rodosto and sank her as she tied up to the quay, then forced a fourth victim to run ashore before making good his escape. Nasmith's most famous feat was penetrating Constantinople roads and sinking the transport *Stamboul* as she lay at the wharfside embarking stores. Frustrated, like Stoker and Boyle before him, by *E11*'s lack of a gun, Nasmith developed an extremely hazardous technique for eking out his dwindling stock of torpedoes. Each torpedo was set to float at the end of its run. If a torpedo missed, Nasmith would track it down, then personally swim across and unscrew the firing pistol from the warhead. The torpedo would then be guided back into *E11*'s stern tube and prepared for another shot.

Both Boyle and Nasmith (each of whom won the VC) returned to the Marmara after their boats had gone to Malta to have guns fitted. This improvement made to the five submarines which operated in the Marmara throughout the later months of 1915 reduced Turkish seaborne traffic to *dhows* and forced the Turks to withdraw all their surviving warships to the Black

Sea. Inevitably, there were casualties. *E7* was caught and destroyed in the strengthened net defences of the Dardanelles on 4 September; *E20* was ambushed and sunk by the newly arrived German submarine *UB-14* on 21 October 1914.

For all their tactical brilliance, the British submarines in the Marmara achieved little of strategic value. Germany's submarine build-up in the southern theatre from August 1915 proved capable of snatching the initiative in the Mediterranean even before the British evacuated Gallipoli in December 1915–January 1916. Hersing moved up to Varna on the Black Sea coast and was reinforced with 'UB' and 'UC' boats to operate against the Russians in the Black Sea and the British in the Marmara. (*UB-14*'s sinking of *E20* was one of the first successes of Hersing's half-flotilla.) In August 1915 four more U-boats—*U-33*, *U-34*, *U-35* and *U-39*, with *U-38* joining in November—were sent to the Adriatic to operate from Cattaro against Anglo-French shipping in the Mediterranean. And it was one of the latter, *U-35*, which became the most successful submarine of all time under command of the U-boat 'ace of aces', Lothar Arnauld de la Perière.

From the time she commissioned in November 1914 to the Armistice four years later, *U-35* sank 224 merchant ships totalling 535,900 tons. Of these, over 83 percent—189 ships, totalling 446,708 tons—were sunk between November 1915 and March 1918, when Arnauld de la Perière commanded *U-35*. His record month was 26 July–20 August 1916, when he sank 54 ships totalling 91,000 tons. But Arnauld de la Perière's achievement did not depend on the use of the submarine as an undersea weapon. It was, rather, the masterly exploitation of the contemporary *weaknesses* of the submarine as a weapons system. If Arnauld de la Perière had relied on submerged torpedo attacks his count of victims could never have mounted so spectacularly. But he was an exponent of the careful periscope reconnaissance followed by a sudden gun action on the surface. Brilliant loner that he was, he handled *U-35* as a submersible surface raider. And he was most

Below: A U-boat takes on more shells between cruises.

generously assisted by the failure of the Allies to devise a sane anti-submarine programme. Instead the French and British persisted in sailing merchantmen along fixed routes, escorted by warships whose responsibility for their charges ended abruptly on the boundary of each command zone. There were 18 such zones, each one jealously autonomous and indifferent to its neighbours' fortunes. It was easy for the U-boats to dodge the scattered patrols, and the situation remained so until the Allies belatedly came to their senses and began to sail their ships in protective convoys.

The Germans began 1916 with 58 operational U-boats and a wealth of most promising experience. As the British still had no effective anti-submarine weapons or tactics this was the moment, hindsight argues, when Germany should have taken the plunge and staked all on an unrestricted U-boat campaign. But Bethmann Hollweg still feared that such a move, with the inevitable American casualties it would inflict, would goad the United States into joining the Allies. For 1916—as they had done in August 1914 and would do again in March 1918—the Germans put their faith in a land offensive, the objective in 1916 being to 'bleed the French Army white' at Verdun. Once the French had been rendered incapable of further effort, 'that breaking point would be reached and England's best sword knocked out of her hand'. To accompany the Verdun offensive, which opened on 21 February 1916, the U-boat campaign against Britain was resumed, but carefully. In an absurd compromise, the undersea war was to be simultaneously intensified and held in check.

The instructions to U-boats issued on 13 March ordered that all merchantmen encountered in the war zone were to be sunk, and those encountered outside to be sunk only if they were armed. Passenger steamers (armed or not) were not to be attacked by submerged submarines—which, in practice, meant not at all. Briefly, British merchant shipping losses soared again, with 37 ships (126,000 tons) sunk in April. By June 1916 British merchant-ship losses had fallen off to 16 ships (36,000 tons) for the month. But the summer of 1916 was the last time that the British Admiralty was able to cling to the delusion that the fall-off in sinkings was due to defensive measures. From September the submarine campaign began again, and this time it would not be suspended but would escalate into the unrestricted offensive for which the U-boat protagonists had never ceased to agitate. Their campaign began.

As 1917 opened, the year in which the U-boats would come closer to defeating Britain than any element of the German armed forces was to do in either of the world wars, the deadly statistics for the world's first unrestricted submarine campaign had already been drafted. They all revolved round tonnage—the tonnage of merchant ships which the British must keep flowing in order to stay in the war—and the number of operational U-boats available to sink it. If the U-boats sank more merchant tonnage than the German Navy lost U-boats, the British were bound to lose. Conversely, if the British could preserve (or replace) enough merchant tonnage, and sink enough U-boats in the process, they would survive—and so would the grinding blockade being inflicted on Germany, which the German High Command knew full well was bound to strangle the German war effort if not thrown off.

The U-boats came close to victory because the British took so long in deciding to sail their merchant ships in convoy and to mass-produce depth-charges—the deadliest anti-submarine weapon produced in World War I.

The British survived because the Germans had based their calculations on the ease of sinking large numbers of independently routed merchantmen, but had developed no tactics for systematic attacks on convoys.

At the beginning of 1917, the Germans had 138 U-boats in commission, including 'UB' and 'UC' types. During the unrestricted campaign, which opened on 1 February, only about 40 would be at sea on any given day and half of those would be heading home for repairs and replenishment. (The monthly average number at sea between August 1914 and January 1917 had been 12.) But given the Allied shipping weaknesses which prevailed until the adoption of convoy, there were enough U-boats to inflict the following losses on the British alone:

1917 (month)	*Ships sunk (British)*	*Tons*
January	35	109,954
February	86	256,394
March	103	283,647
April	155	516,394

As the U-boat offensive was accompanied by a stepped-up mining programme and the efforts of three elusive surface raiders disguised as merchantmen, British shipping losses were, by the end of April, fast approaching the monthly

level which the Germans had calculated would guarantee Britain's collapse. The German objective was the sinking of 600,000 tons per month and the permanent frightening-off of the 1,200,000 tons of neutral shipping on which the Allies depended. But, as tends to happen with issues of such magnitude and novelty, both sides got their sums wrong.

The main reason why the British delayed their vital adoption of the convoy system until May 1917 was that the Admiralty believed it to be an impossible task. This negative attitude was erroneously based on a set of figures which suggested that there were far too many merchantmen at sea on any given day to be sailed and escorted in convoy. These were the customs returns, which showed the coming and going of vessels of every nationality over 100 tons—many of which, coasters and cross-Channel streamers, were counted several times per week. But the figure that mattered was the amount of ocean-going steamers over 1000 tons arriving and departing every week. Not until early April was it revealed that there were only about 140 of such ships, coming and going, 280 in all—not 5000-odd.

The Admiralty only had a few weeks to digest this radically different prospect before Prime Minister Lloyd George, breathing fire and insisting that the convoy strategy be adopted at once, descended on the Admiralty on 30 April 1917. Though this must be accounted one of the most timely political interventions in naval history, Lloyd George was not solely responsible for the adoption of the convoy system: he merely gave the spur to the reversal of over two and a half years of opposition, born of rigid bureaucracy inside the Admiralty and failure to define the problem correctly.

The Germans were equally let down by their own miscalculations. Though they accepted that unrestricted U-boat warfare would probably bring in the Americans on the Allied side (as it did on 6 April 1917), they also believed that the United States had little of any immediate military value to contribute, and that the Allies could be forced into a negotiated peace before the United States was fully geared up for war. Above all the Germans believed that neutral countries would be permanently deterred from sailing cargoes to British ports. This did not happen. After six months—by which time the Germans had calculated that the British would be at their breaking-point—neutral shipping to

The first weapon in the counterattack against submerged submarines was the hydrophone, here shown in use on the British trawler *Thrive*. But without sonar to confirm range and bearing, all the hydrophone could do was to notify escort vessels when there were engine noises where no engine noises ought to be.

Britain was back at 80 percent of its normal volume and the British had rushed through a totally new programme of shipping construction and dockyard repairs—another feature of earlier complacency and neglect for whose correction the Germans had not bargained.

Moreover, the Germans believed that they were sinking far more tonnage than they actually were. This was due primarily to human error on the part of the U-boat captains who, under the immense stress of the campaign, tended to over-estimate the tonnage of their victims (just as, in 1940, RAF Fighter Command pilots were to over-estimate the numbers of German aircraft they shot down). But the biggest error on the German side was the failure to guess how quickly the Allies could reorganise their hitherto vulnerable shipping, and present the U-boats with the insuperable problem of escorted convoys.

The adoption of the convoy principle swept merchantmen together into formation; the scrapping of the futile 'anti-submarine patrols', which the U-boats had always found so easy to dodge, provided the convoy's escort warships. Now, instead of picking off isolated victims one by one, U-boats had to hunt for these big defensive formations in order to maintain their tonnage quotas. Here British radio interception proved invaluable. A U-boat reporting its position to base would be 'overheard' in London; the convoy commodore would be alerted and the convoy swung away from the ambush which seemed to be preparing. For U-boats which did make contact with convoys, keeping in touch imposed terrific strain on the crews and every attack invited an instant counterattack by the escorts.

Painfully developed throughout 1915 and distributed in tiny numbers from early 1916, the depth-charge was a bomb fired by a hydrostatic detonator, which operated as soon as the charge had sunk to a pre-selected depth. A near-

Below: *Wasserbomb!* An American destroyer carries out a depth-charge attack. Opposite: *U-22* demonstrates that submarines are no less vulnerable to mines than surface craft. When she had her stern blown off by a mine in April 1917, *U-22* was lucky that the explosion did not detonate the warheads of the torpedoes in her two stern tubes (centre) or of the two reloads (outboard).

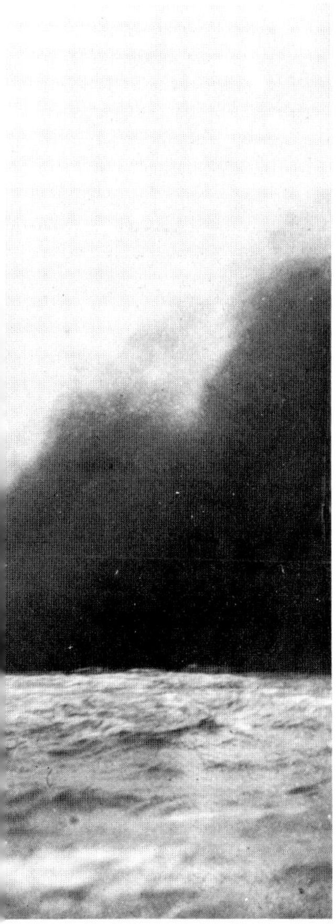

miss could destroy a U-boat, and anything between about 14 and 28 feet usually caused so much damage that the U-boat would be forced to surface. The strain of awaiting a depth-charge attack, as the noise of the hunter's screws welled to crescendo and passed overhead, followed by the thunderous concussion of the charges, had to be repeatedly endured as the U-boats strove to come to grips with the convoys. This was grimly summed up by future U-boat supremo Karl Dönitz, whose last World War I command (in the Mediterranean, where convoy was also introduced) was *U-68*:

> 'The oceans at once became bare and empty; for long periods at a time the U-boats, operating individually, would see nothing at all; and then, suddenly, up would loom a huge concourse of ships, thirty or fifty or more of them, surrounded by an escort of warships of all types. The solitary U-boat, which most probably had sighted the convoy purely by chance, would then attack, thrusting again and again and persisting, if the commander had strong nerves, for perhaps several days and nights, until the physical exhaustion of both commander and crew called a halt. The lone U-boat might well sink one or two of the ships, or even several, but that was a poor percentage of the whole.'

Though the first experimental convoys started to run in May 1917 it took another two months before any genuine easement was felt; but the fall-off in losses to U-boat attack from the terrible April of 1917 tells its own story:

1917 (month)	*Ships sunk (British)*	*Tons*
April	155	516,394
May	106	320,572
June	116	417,925
July	88	319,931
August	84	310,551
September	68	173,437
October	79	261,649
November	56	154,806

Thus within six months of the slaughter inflicted in April 1917, the U-boats were already sinking 50 percent less tonnage and their unrestricted campaign had clearly failed to knock Britain out of the war. The new Atlantic convoys were not as big as Dönitz so gloomily claimed; the largest, sailed in June 1918, numbered 47 ships and the average size was in the region of 20–25 ships. But the convoys *did* sweep most of the easy victims off the sealanes, driving the U-boats closer and closer inshore. Down to July 1917 55 percent of sinkings had taken place over 50 miles from land; by December 1917 this had fallen off to eight percent. Altogether—from May 1917 to the Armistice in November 1918—16,070 ships sailed in ocean convoys and only 96 were sunk by U-boats: a mere 0.6 percent. When convoy was extended into British coastal and inshore waters in 1918 the results were even more gratifying: 0.24 percent sunk, or only 161 out of 67,888 ships convoyed in coastal waters down to the Armistice.

Part of the reason for the baffling of the U-boats was the fact that escort warships were always on hand to 'chase down' any U-boat which tried to attack a convoy. But the biggest virtue of convoy was that it prevented U-boats from doing what they had always had to do in order to make sure of a sinking: finish off their victims on the surface, either with gunfire or by boarding and placing explosive charges. A torpedoed ship now had an excellent chance of being taken in tow and brought safely to port, where improved repair facilities were waiting to send the stricken vessel quickly back to sea. Meanwhile, as likely as not, the U-boat com-

Above: *Deutschland* dressed overall for her American cruise.

A ticklish moment aboard *U-35*. Swaying over a replacement torpedo before easing its ungainly bulk down through the submarine's fore-hatch was a job which, if carried out at sea, as here, definitely called for calm seas and a steady boat.

mander would have gone home claiming a torpedo hit and probable sinking—if he survived. Though U-boat losses never rose so high as to force a suspension of operations—as they were to do in the summer of 1943—more and more boats were being lost by the end of 1917. Sixty-five U-boats were sunk that year, 44 of them between July and December. By the end of the year, for the first time in the war, U-boat losses were approaching the construction rate of new boats and in some months actually surpassing it. In November and December 1917, for instance, 16 U-boats were lost and only 11 new ones were commissioned.

The defeat of the U-boats in 1917, however, was primarily due to the strictly defensive measure of convoy—not to any new Allied weaponry or tactics, or to the rising losses being inflicted on the U-boat arm.

Though the battle was confined mainly to the eastern Atlantic, Britain's Western Approaches and the Mediterranean, the Germans made one innovation which boded ill for the future. This was the deployment of long-range submarines capable of cruising to the American coast and back: the spectacular, outsize 'U-cruisers', displacing over 1500 tons and armed with a brace of 5.9-inch guns as well as bow torpedo tubes.

The U-cruisers were developed from the submarine merchantmen produced as an experimental counter to the British blockade, the first of which, *Deutschland*, made two propaganda trading voyages to the United States in 1916. When converted and armed as *U-155*, *Deutschland* made a maiden war cruise lasting

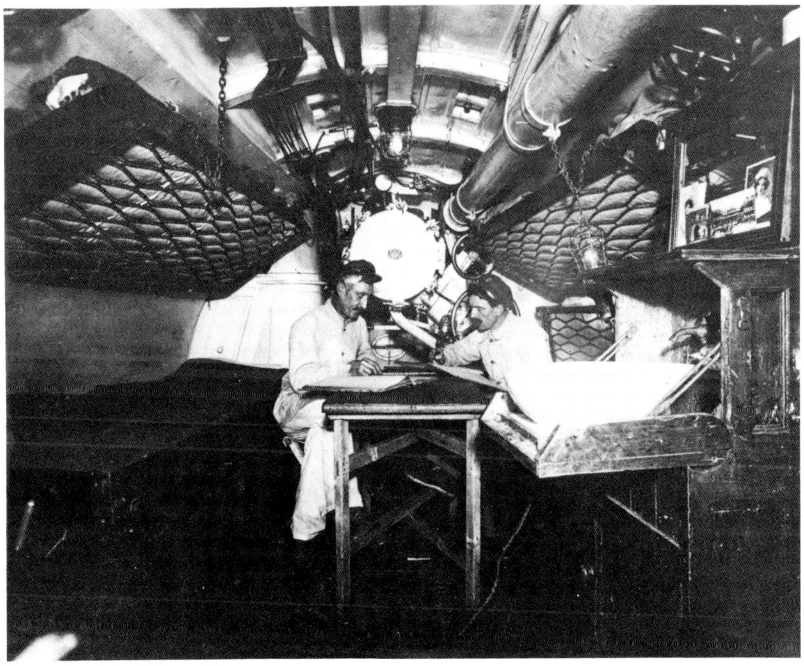

from 24 May to 4 September 1917 in which she sank ten steamers and seven sailing ships—nearly 52,000 tons of British, Allied and neutral shipping. Six others were converted and rushed into service, and over 30 more were ordered (thus adding considerably to the production problems of the more proven types). But the U-cruisers, like Arnauld de la Perière's *U-35*, were really a demonstration of the tactical weaknesses of World War I submarines: they were intended to intimidate and crush resistance *on the surface*, using gun-power. Operating alone they could never succeed in breaking up a convoy into defenceless individuals. Their initial successes came in the early days of the convoy system, before American participation enabled convoys to be run all the way across the Atlantic with adequate warship escort.

The shape of things to come was glimpsed by Hermann Bauer, commander of the U-boat arm since the beginning of the war. He suggested using the U-cruisers as command and supply ships for combined submarine attacks on the convoys, guiding U-boats to the target by radio in liaison with shore headquarters. This was overruled as far as U-cruiser operations were concerned, and although experiments in U-boat co-ordination were made it was found that radio communication was still too primitive to give the idea a fair trial. Bauer, who had done a magnificent job as commander of the U-boat arm since 1914, was replaced by *Kommodore* Andreas Michelsen in June 1917. Individual U-boat commanders, however, did pioneer the tactic of combined submarine attack, most notably Karl Dönitz in *U-68*. On 4 October 1918 *U-68* and *U-48* were pressing home an attack on a Mediterranean convoy when *U-68* was so badly damaged that Dönitz had to scuttle her and surrender. But this personal failure and humiliation did not persuade him that combined attack—*rudeltaktik*, or the 'wolf pack' concept—was a mistaken idea. In World War II he was to perfect it with deadly effect.

By the spring of 1918 the U-boats were still enough of a menace for the British to make their famous attempt to seal off the Bruges canal at Zeebrugge with blockships (22–23 April), in an attempt to curtail the operations of the Flanders Flotilla. Despite the high gallantry of the attackers the little 'UB' class boats were still able to squeeze past the blockships. The U-boat arm, numbering 123 operational boats at the beginning of the year, lost another 83 before the Armistice while only 80 new boats were completed. But the dedication of the German submariners, right to the last, was demonstrated by the exploit of *UB-116* (*Kapitänleutnant* Kurt Emsmann), barely three weeks before the Armistice.

In late October 1918 Emsmann embarked on a lone mission to penetrate Scapa Flow, a desperate attempt to prove that the German Navy still had teeth, and so improve Germany's bargaining position during the armistice negotiations. It was a grim demonstration of how much things had changed at Scapa since the panicky days of 1914. The Flow was now ringed with electrically triggered minefields, hydrophones and magnetic detectors to indicate when a submarine was passing over the mines. As Emsmann took *UB-116* into Hoxa Sound on the night of 28 October, the sound of his electric motors was picked up by the shore hydrophones; the needle on the observer's dial

Top: In the control room of the French submarine *Andromaque*. Beneath the periscope is the well into which the instrument descends when lowered. Above: Spacious crew quarters in the *Montgolfier*.

74
D.4

Gun armament proceeds from the sublime to the ridiculous. Left: *D4*, the first British submarine to carry a gun. Below and right: The 'submarine monitor' *M1*, with her monstrous 12-inch gun.

flickered as *UB-116* crossed a controlled minefield; a switch was thrown and a row of exploding mines sank *UB-116* with all hands.

When the world's first undersea war ended with the Armistice on 11 November 1918, all the indications were that the Allies had learned more in defence than the Germans had learned in attack. Convoy was the foundation of survival, with the massed merchantmen escorted by warships on the surface and, where possible, by aeroplanes and airships aloft. The mass production and distribution of depth-charges had enabled the escorts to counterattack with mounting effectiveness. Above all the ASDIC—the Anglo-French 'Anti-Submarine Detection Investigation Committee'—was already working flat out on the vital problem of detecting submerged submarines, the most important missing piece of the puzzle.

Had the war continued, the Germans would have begun the 1919 campaign with no real answer to the convoy problem. Though 185 U-boats were surrendered intact to the Allies and another 192 had been sunk or scuttled, far too many of them were of the U-cruiser type with its inherent emphasis on surface attack. In the field of 'artificial aids', the most important German discovery had been the value of hydrophones in detecting the approach of surface vessels, and the efficacy of 'silent routine' in foiling hydrophones listening from the noisy surface of the sea. There was little to choose between Allied and German submariners when it came to courage and endurance. But it was the

Above and below: The U-boats surrender. The Germans never learned that an upside-down 'lucky horseshoe' lets the luck run out.

WORLD WAR I: BRITISH MERCHANT SHIPPING LOSSES (Gross tonnage)

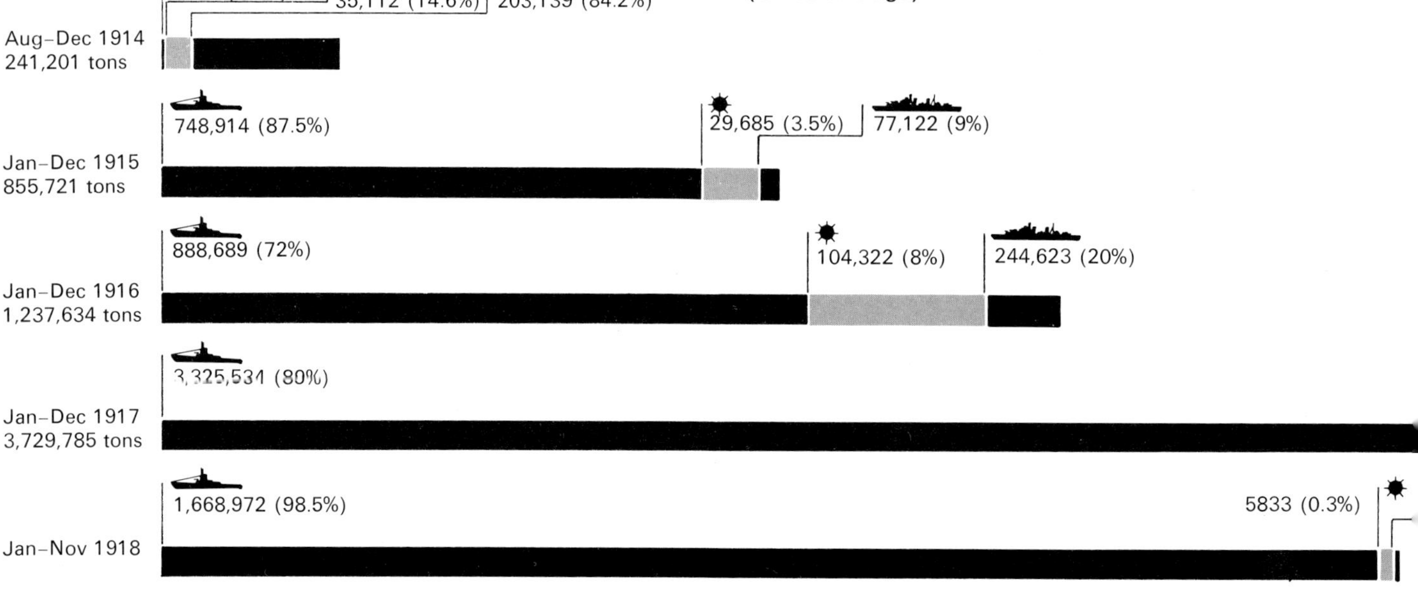

WORLD WAR I: U-BOAT CONSTRUCTION AND LOSSES

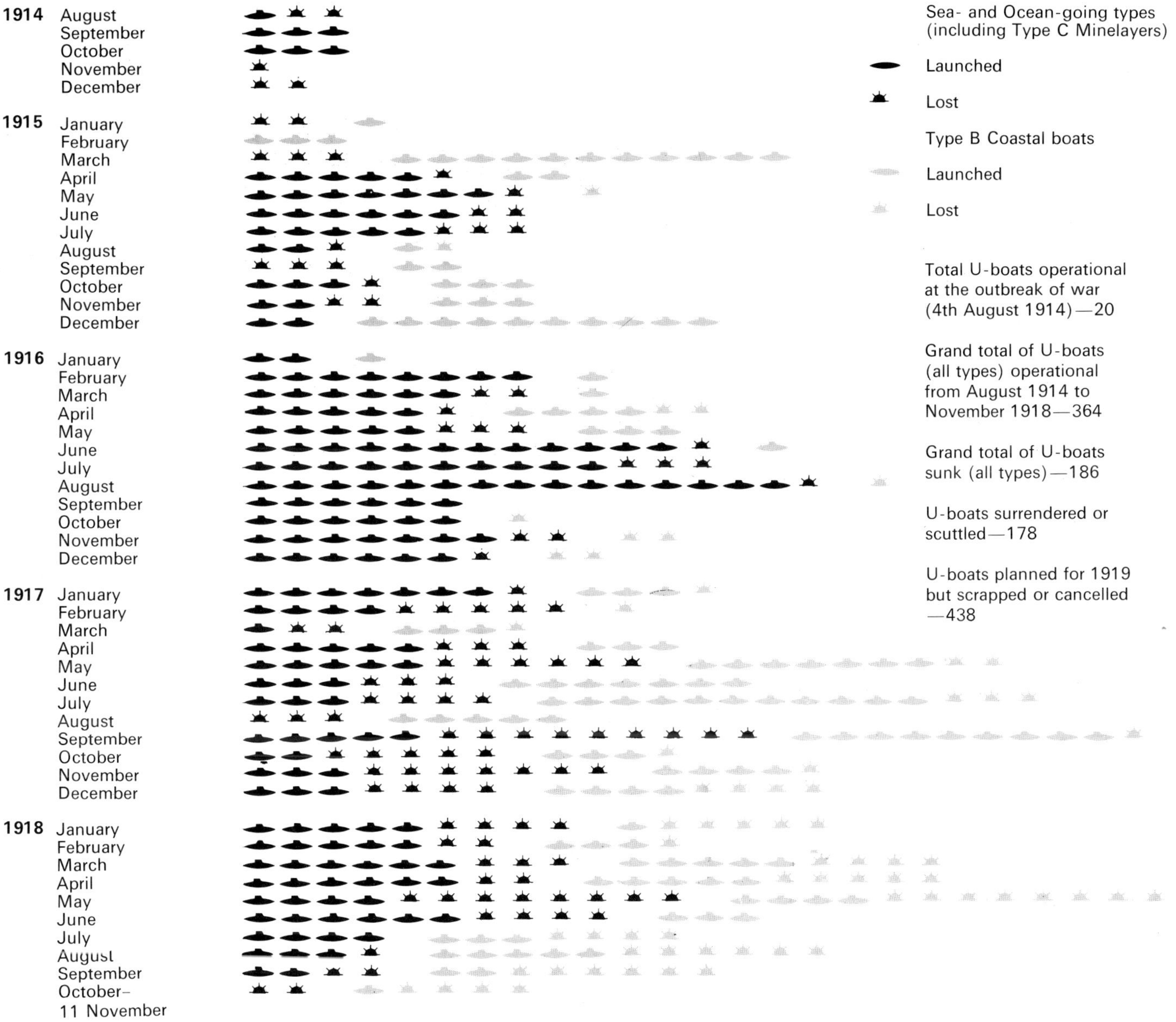

British 'K-ship' (*K2*), one of the most remarkable craft produced in World War I. Steam turbines gave them an impressive surface speed of 24 knots, but a flared clipper bow was needed to prevent the bow being driven under.

German submarine arm which had introduced unrestricted submarine commerce war, proving the latter to be as deadly a potential war-winner as has ever been devised.

Literally the biggest phenomenon of World War I submarine development was the big submarine cruiser, designed for long-range patrols lasting a couple of months or more. This, the forerunner of the modern nuclear submarine, was inadequate in 1916–18 only in that its contemporary weaponry and machinery kept it shackled to the surface. The British experimented with submarine cruisers—the wartime 'K' ships and later 'M' class submarine monitors, the latter preposterously armed with a single 12 inch gun each. But all these proved was that large submarines were feasible; the experience of World War I had proved that submarines should not be tied down or made to manoeuvre as part of a surface fleet. Tactically, the submarine cruiser was a waste; it could do nothing that surface ships could not do better except submerge, thus rendering its dominant (gun) weapons useless. The British sensibly abandoned submarine cruisers after *M1* sank in a Channel collision in 1925 and *M2* foundered in 1932; but the French went on to complete *Surcouf*, then the world's biggest submarine, in 1934. Though designed as a merchant raider, she proved in World War II to have no fully effective role.

Another fruit of World War I submarine development years ahead of its time was the specialised anti-submarine submarine—the type known today as the 'hunter-killer'. Operating as they were from the defensive, the British introduced the 'hunter-killer' in 1918, in the form of the 'R' class boats. Highly streamlined, the 'R' boats were the first submarines capable of greater speeds submerged (15 knots) than when surfaced (9.5 knots). They were not to be surpassed until the German Type XXI boats at the end of World War II. Between the wars, submarine development inevitably suffered from

peacetime defence cuts and the lack of impetus. To the victorious Allied sea powers in 1919 it seemed enough to prohibit Germany from retaining or ever building submarines again. The League of Nations predictably denounced unrestricted submarine warfare as an outrage against civilisation, reaffirming the pre-1914 Hague Convention Prize Laws. This cannot be written off as wishful thinking in the light of previous experience, for there was similar wishful thinking behind the rebirth of a German U-boat force in the middle 1930s. When the German Navy began to rearm in the late 1920s it did so under the comforting assumption—confirmed by Chancellor Hitler's original assurances to Grand-Admiral Raeder in 1933—that Germany would never fight Britain again. By 1938–39, five years after the first 250-ton 'Type 2' U-boats had been laid down, it was a different story. The German naval 'Z Plan' of January 1939 aimed at building a balanced fleet—battleships, aircraft-carriers, cruisers, destroyers and 250 submarines—scheduled for completion between 1944 and 1948.

The outbreak of war in 1939 bore no comparison to that of 1914, for there was no German masterplan for a war against France and Britain as well as Poland. Hitler's invasion of Poland landed him with a conflict for which his armed forces were wholly unprepared. On the first day of World War II Karl Dönitz, commander of the still diminutive U-boat force, spelled out his position in a memorandum of admirable clarity:

> 'With 22 boats and a prospective increase of one to two boats a month I am incapable of undertaking efficacious measures against England.'

It only remained to be seen how prepared were the victors of 1918 to undertake efficacious measures against the U-boats.

Above: Airship 'Submarine Scout Zero' comes in to land on HMS *Furious* in 1918. Before the development of aircraft-carriers, these 'blimps' provided the first effective air patrols against U-boats. Below: German seaplanes attack British submarine *C25* off Harwich (6 July 1918). Bombs and machine-gun fire killed the British captain and five ratings, preventing *C25* from diving. Despite a second air attack she was eventually towed into port by another submarine (*E51*).

1939–1945

The most enduring myth about Nazi Germany and the outbreak of World War II is the belief that in September 1939 Germany was armed to the teeth and all set for world conquest. In fact none of the German armed forces was ready for anything more ambitious than a 'one-off' campaign against Poland. The Luftwaffe had no heavy bombers. The Army had no heavy tanks and still relied on horse-drawn transport. And the Navy, which in the decade before 1914 had been built up deliberately for a showdown with Britain, had in September 1939 spent most of the prewar decade under the assumption that a second naval confrontation with Britain was out of the question. The construction of a submarine fleet capable of waging another killer offensive against British merchant shipping had scarcely begun, and the Navy's U-boats suffered the same fate as the Luftwaffe's bombers and the Army's tanks. To build up numbers quickly, the decision was made to concentrate production on the medium types already in production at the outset of the war.

Hitler's war strategy was strictly opportunist and he began by being as anxious as the Allies to contain and limit the war, sparing no effort to soothe the apprehension of neutrals. The latent unreality of this policy, under which the U-boats went to war ordered to observe the Prize Regulations, was demonstrated on the first day of the war. On 3 September *Kapitänleutnant* Julius Lemp, patrolling the Western Approaches in *U-30*, torpedoed and sank the British liner *Athenia*. He claimed that he had mistaken her for a troopship. The incident was a propaganda boon to both sides, the Germans replying to British denunciations of the atrocity by asserting that *Athenia* had been sunk by the British to discredit Germany. In practical terms the incident induced the British and French to accelerate the institution of coastal and oceanic convoys.

Below: Close-up of *U-38*'s conning-tower, her crew at attention as she passes Grand-Admiral Raeder in review after one of her first war patrols in October 1939. *U-38* and *U-37* were the only two of the eight Type IXA boats to survive the Battle of the Atlantic; both were scuttled in German waters on 5 May 1945.

When Britain and France declined to make peace after the defeat of Poland, restrictions on U-boat operations were progressively lifted from 23 September until, on 17 November, they were allowed to attack liners without warning 'if clearly identifiable as hostile'. Though there never was a formal German proclamation of unrestricted submarine warfare, as there had been in 1917, the latter had in fact come into being in the first two months of the war, preceded by its antidote: convoy. Here at least was one respect in which the lessons of World War I had been learned and applied within the opening months of World War II.

Down to the end of 1939 the U-boats' main prey was the host of unescorted merchantmen caught overseas by the outbreak of war and making lone runs for home. As these could not be given the protection of convoy, their losses, though high, would have been even higher if Dönitz had had more U-boats at sea. Between September and December 1939 114 British, Allied and neutral merchantmen fell victim to U-boats (421,156 tons in all), only four of them in convoy. These casualties were predictable. A far bigger worry by November and December 1939 was the rapidly mounting toll of sinkings in British coastal waters, caused by the first German 'secret weapon' to be unleashed in the war: the magnetic mine. Laid on the sea bed in shallow coastal waters, this weapon was detonated by a ship's magnetic field passing overhead and could not be swept by conventional means. In November and December 1939, when the U-boats accounted for only 47 merchantmen, 59 ships were sunk by mines. But when a magnetic mine was accidentally dropped on a tidal mud flat exposed at low water (23 November) the British were able to dismantle the weapon, discover its polarity and develop effective countermeasures. Without this piece of luck the magnetic mine (of which only about 1500 had been manufactured by the outbreak of war) could well have succeeded in paralysing convoy traffic between Britain's east coast ports and the Thames estuary.

For Dönitz and his U-boat captains, however, the biggest query in the opening weeks of the war was the effectiveness of the loudly pro-

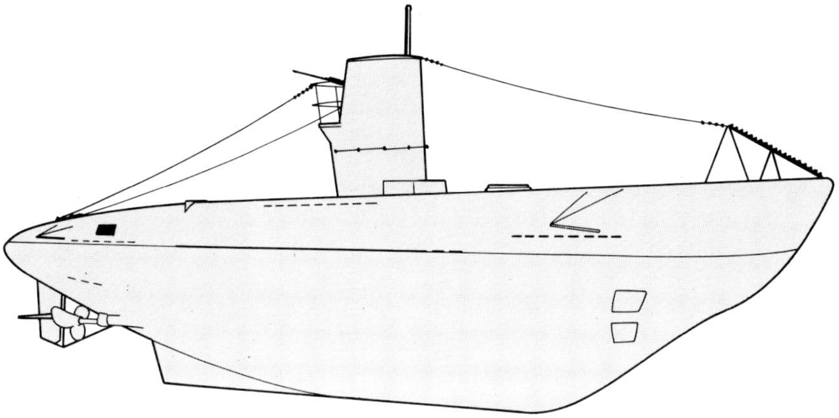

claimed British device for locating submerged submarines. This was known as 'asdic', using the initials of the Anti-Submarine Detection Investigation Committee originally formed in 1917. Mounted beneath a ship's hull, asdic (or 'sonar', as it is known today and will be so termed in this book) sends a regular sonic pulse or 'ping' echoing through the water in a cone-shaped beam. This can be swung from side to side to enable a wider search to be made. When a submarine is found by the beam the 'ping' comes back with an echo which, unless the submarine gets clear of the beam like an aeroplane escaping from a searchlight, enables the hunter to track down the submarine and attack. The development of a workable sonar system in the second half of the 1930s was the vital breakthrough in undersea war; but the British Naval Staff was being wildly optimistic when it reported in 1937 that 'the submarine should never again be able to present us with the problem we were faced with in 1917'.

It was not yet appreciated that the effectiveness of sonar depended on trained operators who had developed an indefinable extra sense; a special 'ear' which told them at once when a 'contact' was a submarine and not a shoal of fish. It also depended on escort commanders able to 'out-think' the submarine skipper they were hunting, and on close, sometimes intuitive teamwork between escorts. Not all of this experience could be built up in peacetime exercises; it could only be fully attained at sea in wartime. Moreover, in September 1939 the fitting of sonar to every warship in the Royal Navy was only just getting under way.

The limited reach of early sonar made it no more than a tool enabling defensive escorts to counterattack, but the British began World War II by repeating their original mistake of the last war, and tried to use it offensively. They patrolled likely U-boat hunting-grounds with aircraft carriers escorted by destroyers fitted with sonar and this, as soon transpired, was a profligate risk. On 14 September *Ark Royal*'s hunting group blundered across *U-39*, which fired four torpedoes at the carrier. Only the fact that the torpedoes' magnetic pistols detonated prematurely saved *Ark Royal* and betrayed *U-39*'s presence to the destroyers, which closed in amid a flurry of depth-charge attacks. Too damaged to escape, *U-39* surfaced and her crew surrendered—the first U-boat lost in the war. But only three days later the U-boats got their revenge. On 17 September *Kapitänleutnant* Otto Schuhart in *U-29* was stalking a merchantman in the St George's Channel when he sighted the carrier *Courageous*. He stalked his new prey for over two hours without being detected either by the escorts' sonar or the carrier's aircraft, then sank *Courageous* with three torpedoes. The escorting destroyers failed to locate *U-29*, which escaped, having given the British a salutary lesson that sonar still had its

Top: Type IIB U-boat.
Above: An easy daylight kill on the surface. The U-boat has been trimmed down with only the upper casing awash, to ensure the torpedo an undisturbed run below the surface.

limitations. Aircraft carriers were promptly withdrawn from the anti-U-boat patrols.

Determined to gain the moral initiative, as the first U-boats had done at the outset of World War I, Dönitz planned an audacious coup: the penetration of Scapa Flow by a lone U-boat. After 20 years of increasing neglect and peacetime economies the Flow's defences were a pale ghost of what they had been in 1918. Dönitz, studying World War I experience and the latest air reconnaisance photographs, correctly deduced that Kirk Sound, east of the Flow, had not been completely sealed with blockships. *Kapitänleutnant* Günther Prien and *U-47* undertook the mission, entered the Flow on the night of 13–14 October, and sank the old battleship *Royal Oak*. Luckily for the British she was the only capital ship there. It was a decided anticlimax for Prien, who disguised the fact in his report and delighted the German propaganda machine with a wonderful tale—how he pressed home his attack, exposed under a sky bright with Northern Lights, then escaped while the Flow sprang to life and hunting destroyers churned up the water with panicky depth-charge attacks. The *Royal Oak* affair was a distasteful and untypical example of a brave and resourceful submariner (Prien was an enthusiastic Nazi, unlike most of his comrades) playing the propagandists' game. Prien's exploit caused the withdrawal of the British Home Fleet from Scapa Flow until the defences could be restored. During the Fleet's absence the battleship *Nelson* and brand-new cruiser *Belfast* were badly damaged by mines.

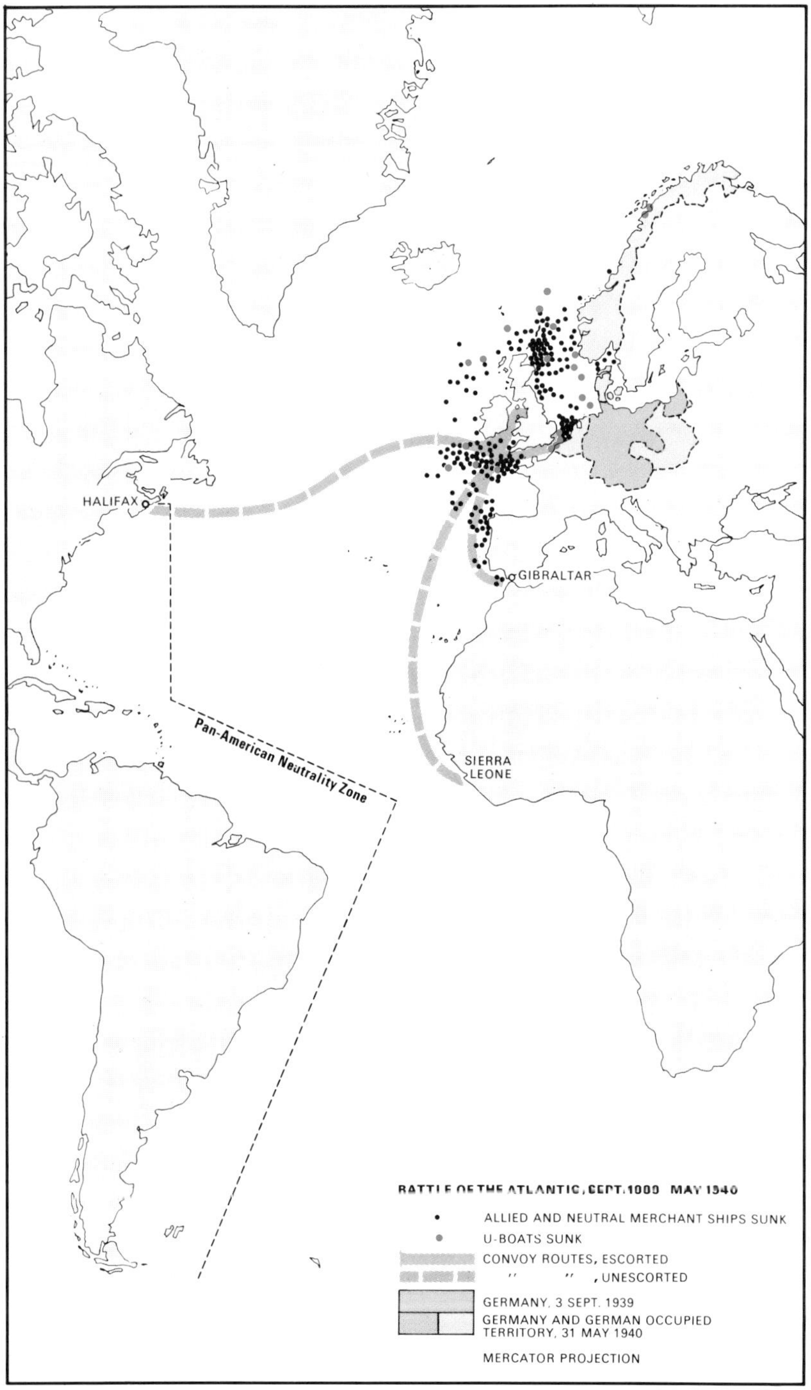

By the end of March 1940 the balance in the U-boat war seemed, if anything, to be tilting in the Allies' favour. Nine U-boats had been sunk in 1939, six of them seagoing Type VIIs suitable for Atlantic cruises. Another five Type VIIs were sunk between January and March 1940, and two of the newer, faster Type IXs. But after April 1940 the balance swung decisively in the Germans' favour. They isolated and corrected the torpedo fault (causing premature explosions or no explosions at all) which plagued the U-boats operating in northern latitudes during the Norwegian campaign (8 April–8 June). On 5 May the British submarine *Seal*, disabled by a mine, was captured in the Kattegat by German seaplanes. She was found to have steel torpedo tubes—a revelation to German designers, who had always taken it for granted that torpedo tubes had to be cast from bronze. The adoption of steel tubes in preference to bronze removed

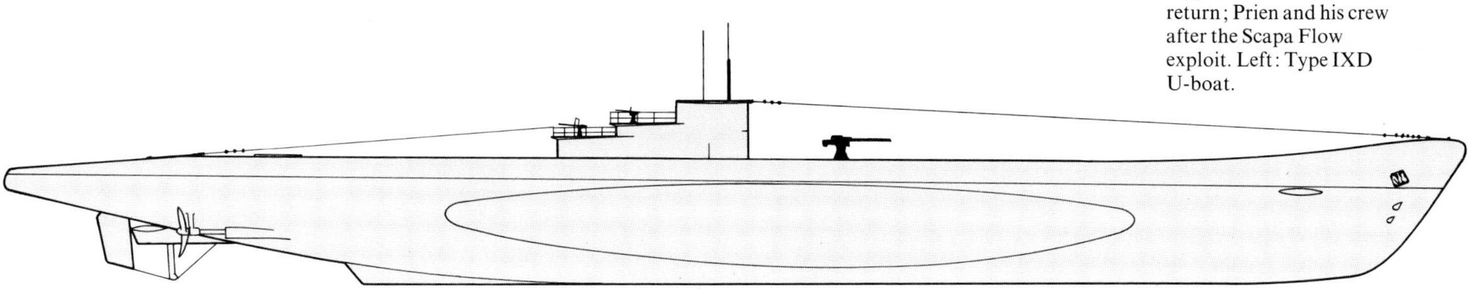

Opposite: The heroes return; Prien and his crew after the Scapa Flow exploit. Left: Type IXD U-boat.

one of the tightest bottlenecks from the U-boat construction programme. But nothing compared to the strategic advantage won by the German land victories between 10 May and 25 June 1940: the conquests not only of Norway but of Holland, Belgium and France. On 7 July *U-30* became the first U-boat to use the Biscay port of Lorient as a supply base, and in late August, before the air battle of Britain had reached its climax, Dönitz moved his operational headquarters from Wilhelmshaven to Lorient.

By the beginning of September 1940 the fortunes of war had so perfectly balanced U-boat losses and new construction that Dönitz had precisely the same number of U-boats as on the first day of the war: 57. The vital difference was that the seagoing Type VIIs and IXs could now be based on the Biscay coast instead of having to make the long outward voyage round the British Isles to reach the Western Approaches. Dönitz could therefore sail enough U-boats at a time to confront every Atlantic convoy to Britain with sustained group attacks by half a dozen U-boats or more. This was the *rudeltaktik* or 'pack tactics' with which he himself had experimented in 1918, and in which he had trained his U-boat commanders. The era of the 'wolf-packs' had began.

Rudeltaktik was simple and flexible. A single U-boat sighting a convoy would tag along, reporting the convoy's size, position and course to Dönitz's headquarters. All U-boats with a chance of intercepting would then be homed on to the convoy. The actual attacks were made on the surface at night. First and foremost, this exploited the simple fact that a submarine's conning-tower is virtually impossible to spot at night, whereas the bulky silhouette of even a blacked-out merchantman stands out against the sky. Second, it rendered the escort's sonar useless, for sonar could not detect *surfaced* submarines. Third, a U-boat running on diesels had the speed with which to keep pace with the convoy, attacking, breaking off and returning

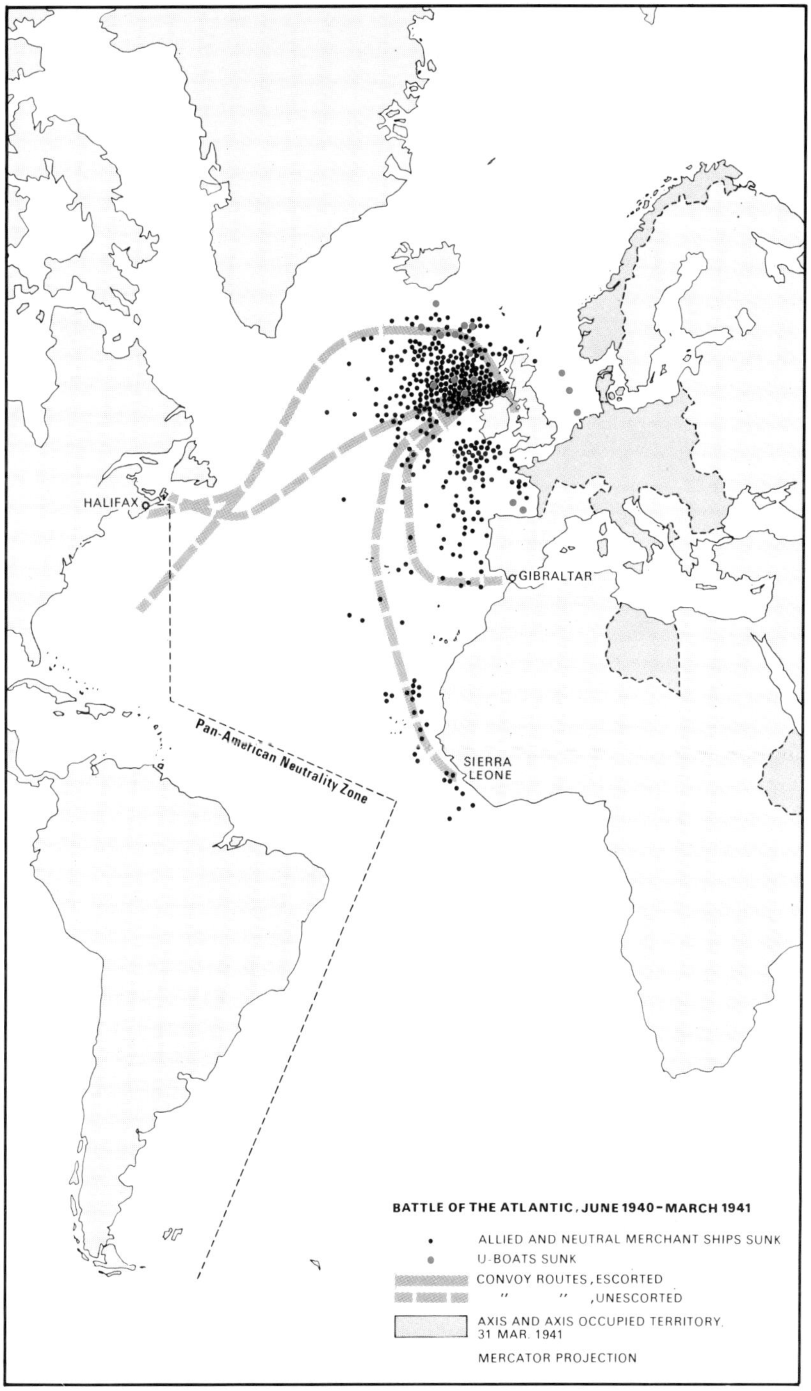

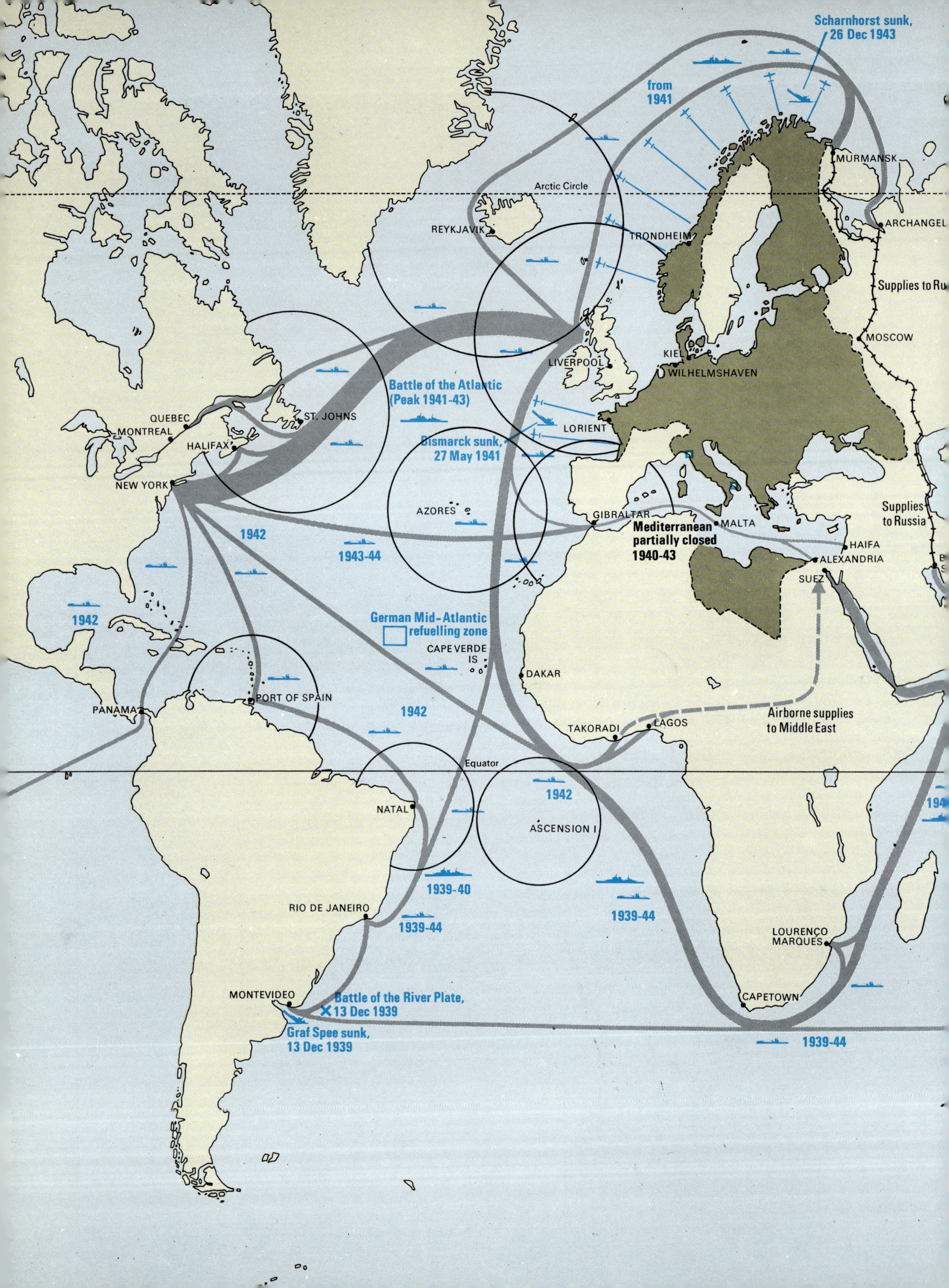

Scharnhorst sunk,
26 Dec 1943
from
1941
MURMANSK
Arctic Circle
ARCHANGEL
REYKJAVIK
TRONDHEIM
Supplies to Ru
MOSCOW
KIEL
WILHELMSHAVEN
LIVERPOOL
Battle of the Atlantic
(Peak 1941-43)
QUEBEC
MONTREAL
ST. JOHNS
HALIFAX
LORIENT
Bismarck sunk,
27 May 1941
NEW YORK
AZORES
GIBRALTAR
MALTA
Mediterranean
partially closed
1940-43
Supplies
to Russia
HAIFA
ALEXANDRIA
SUEZ
1942
1943-44
1942
German Mid-Atlantic
refuelling zone
CAPE VERDE
IS
DAKAR
PORT OF SPAIN
PANAMA
1942
TAKORADI
LAGOS
Airborne supplies
to Middle East
Equator
1942
NATAL
ASCENSION I
1939-40
RIO DE JANEIRO
1939-44
1939-44
LOURENÇO
MARQUES
CAPETOWN
MONTEVIDEO
Battle of the River Plate,
13 Dec 1939
Graf Spee sunk,
13 Dec 1939
1939-44

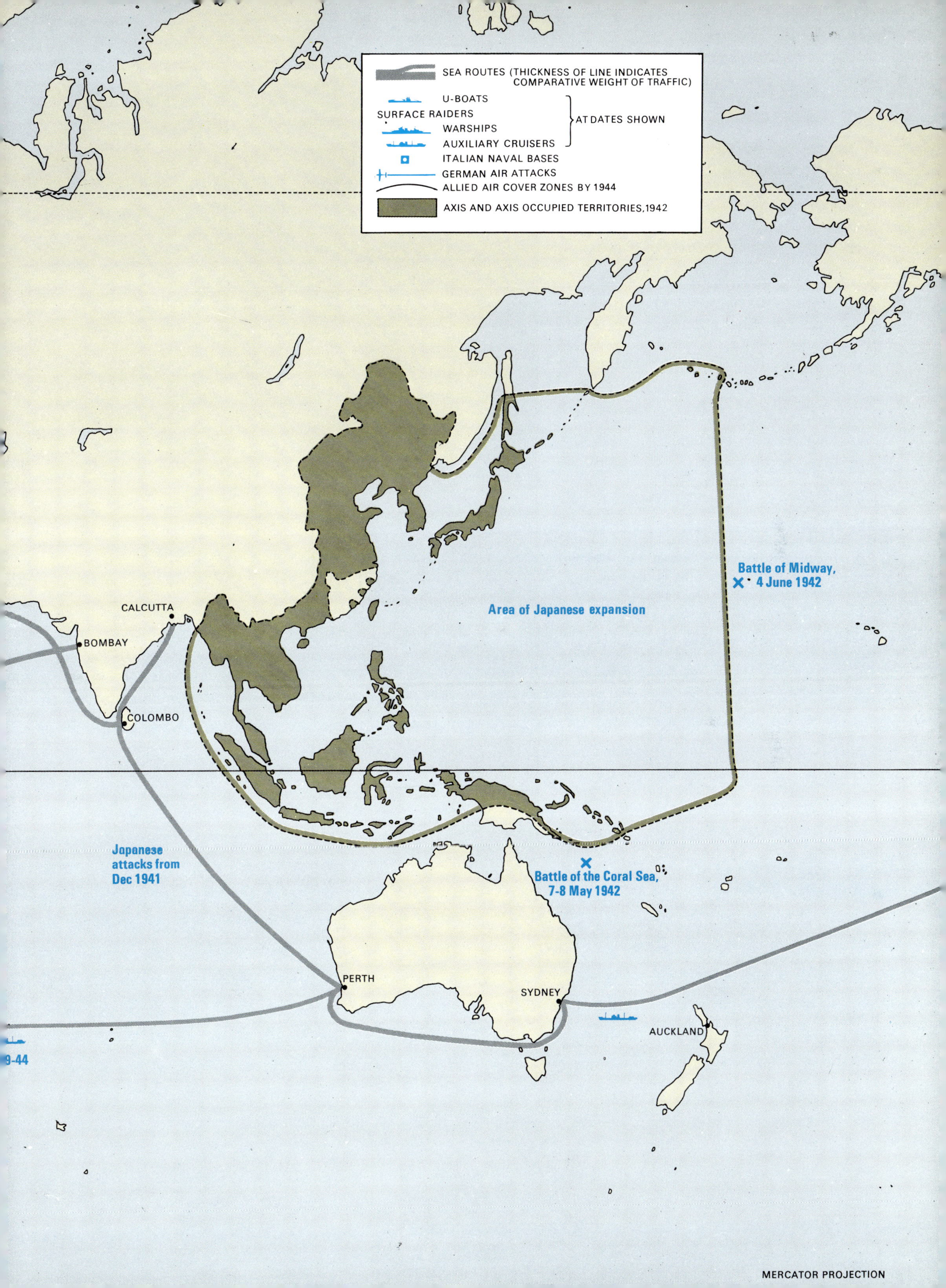

SEA ROUTES (THICKNESS OF LINE INDICATES COMPARATIVE WEIGHT OF TRAFFIC)
U-BOATS
SURFACE RAIDERS
WARSHIPS
AUXILIARY CRUISERS
AT DATES SHOWN
ITALIAN NAVAL BASES
GERMAN AIR ATTACKS
ALLIED AIR COVER ZONES BY 1944
AXIS AND AXIS OCCUPIED TERRITORIES, 1942
CALCUTTA
BOMBAY
COLOMBO
Battle of Midway, 4 June 1942
Area of Japanese expansion
Japanese attacks from Dec 1941
Battle of the Coral Sea, 7-8 May 1942
PERTH
SYDNEY
AUCKLAND
9-44
MERCATOR PROJECTION

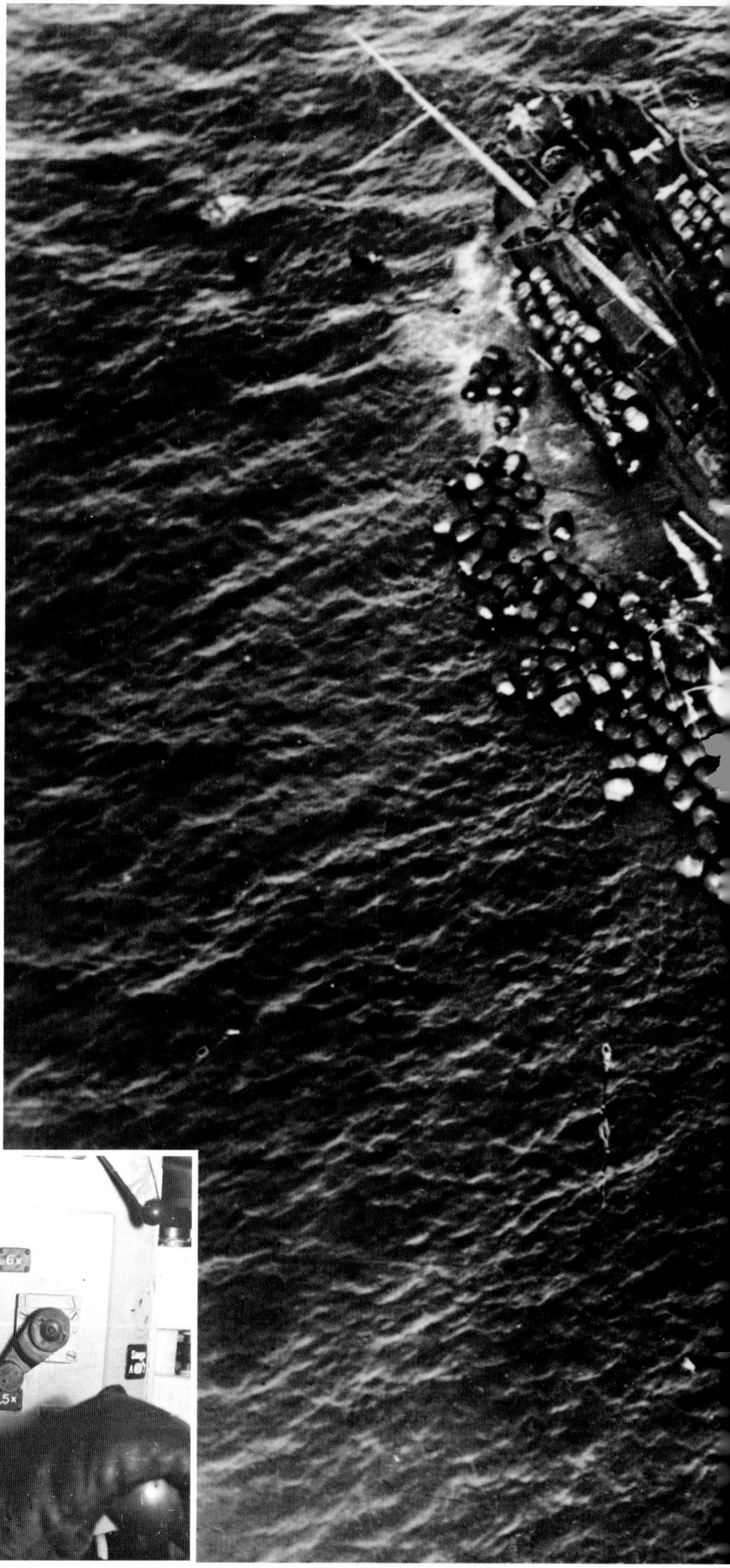

to the attack. A surfaced U-boat could usually outpace anything but a destroyer, and even against a pursuing destroyer a U-boat had a tighter turning circle. Fourth, surfaced action at night enabled the U-boats to keep radio contact with their headquarters, as they could only use their radio when surfaced.

When the new attacks began in September–October 1940 the U-boats had yet another advantage. Peacetime parsimony, the belated reappearance of a German submarine force, and over-confidence in the powers of sonar had left the Royal Navy starved of small warships suited for work as Atlantic convoy escorts. Until the threat of a German invasion receded in October, every available British destroyer was kept in home waters for action against the expected invasion fleet. Thus fast convoys bound for Britain from Halifax (HX) and slow convoys from Sydney, Cape Breton (SC) would sail perhaps with an escort consisting of a single sloop, or armed merchant cruiser. On reaching the meridian of 15° West (the north-south line about 50 miles west of Rockall) HX and SC convoys would be met by escorts from the outward-bound convoys, which were dispersed at this handover point. The resultant scatter of dispersed shipping, stragglers and incoming convoys which had not yet picked up their escorts provided a wolves' banquet for the U-boats—the first 'happy time', as German submariners called it. The British were rushing through an emergency escort-building programme, and begged 50 ancient destroyers from the United States (all of which had to be fitted with sonar before they were of any use against the U-boats). But until these stop-gap escorts joined the battle and reached full combat efficiency the U-boats had things all their own

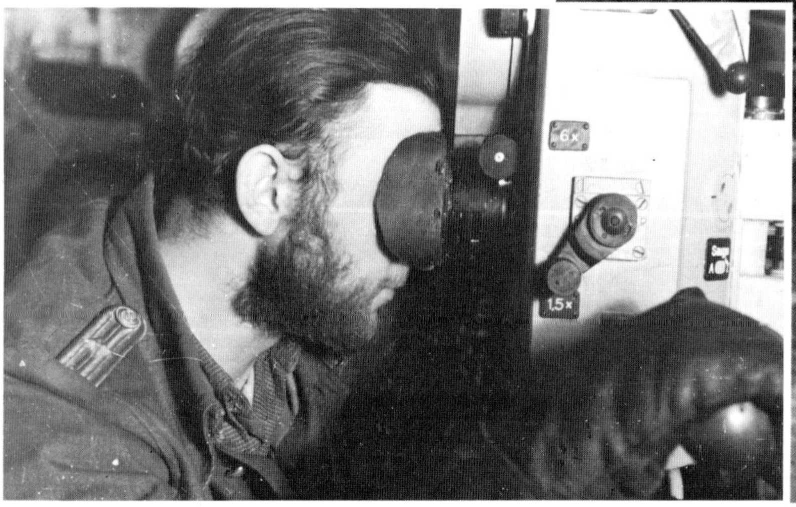

U-boat commander at the periscope (set to low magnification).

Death-throes of a merchantman, rolling helplessly to starboard and spilling her deck cargo of barrels into the sea.

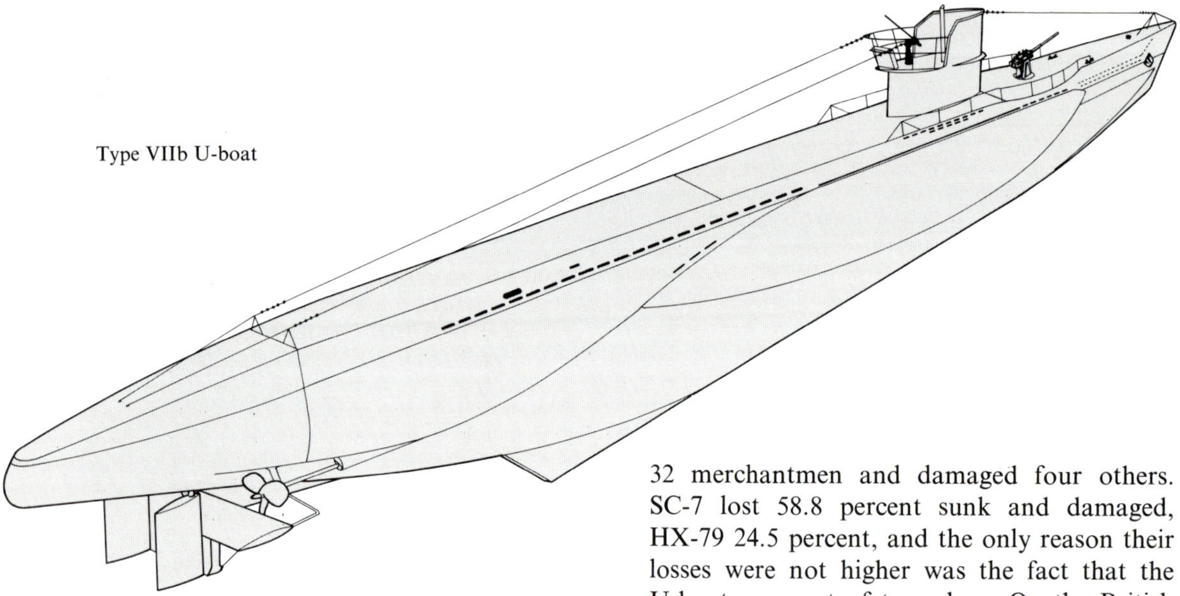

Type VIIb U-boat

way. In October 1940 they sank 63 British, Allied and neutral merchantmen (352,407 tons), 56 of them in the North Atlantic.

Of the many isolated factors which helped save Britain in 1940, three were of particular importance. The first was the unexpected bonus of nearly four million tons of Norwegian, Dutch, Belgian and French merchant shipping which sought refuge in Britain after the German conquest of western Europe. The second was the natural failure of the U-boats to concentrate all their efforts on shipping bound for Britain. They went for the easy meat, the stragglers and dispersed ships, mainly outward bound. These sinkings were no less dangerous to Britain in the long term, but they allowed enough homeward-bound shipping to arrive for Britain to hold on until the foul weather of the winter months caused a fall-off in losses. And the third factor was the uncurbed arrogance and incompetence of *Reichsmarschall* Hermann Göring, overlord of the Luftwaffe, to whom the British really ought to put up a statue. Having failed to prevent the British Army from escaping at Dunkirk, then thrown away victory over RAF Fighter Command in the Battle of Britain, Göring refused to co-operate with the German Navy and release the aircraft needed to set up a German 'fleet air arm'. Insisting that 'everything that flies belongs to me', Göring also refused to place all available long-range reconnaissance and bomber aircraft, particularly suited to scouting over the eastern Atlantic, at the Navy's disposal.

Though starved of the invaluable airborne intelligence which they could have used, the U-boat commanders in October put up a performance which they were never to equal: an average *daily* total of 920 tons sunk. One of their biggest successes was the assault on SC-7 and HX-79 (16–20 October), when six U-boats sank 32 merchantmen and damaged four others. SC-7 lost 58.8 percent sunk and damaged, HX-79 24.5 percent, and the only reason their losses were not higher was the fact that the U-boats ran out of torpedoes. On the British side this double battle was marked by a complete failure to come to grips with the U-boats, despite the apparent strength of the escort (two destroyers, four corvettes, three trawlers and a minesweeper) which met HX-79.

Type VIIc U-boat:
Length 220 feet
Breadth 20 feet
Draught $15\frac{3}{4}$ feet
Surface displacement 769 tons
Maximum speed surfaced 17 knots
Maximum speed submerged 7.6 knots
Endurance surfaced 6,500 miles
Endurance submerged 80 miles
Armament: 5 × 21 inch torpedo tubes, 14 torpedoes
1 × 88mm gun, 1 × 20mm machine gun (after 1943 replaced by 1 × 37mm Flak)
2 twin 20mm Flak machine guns

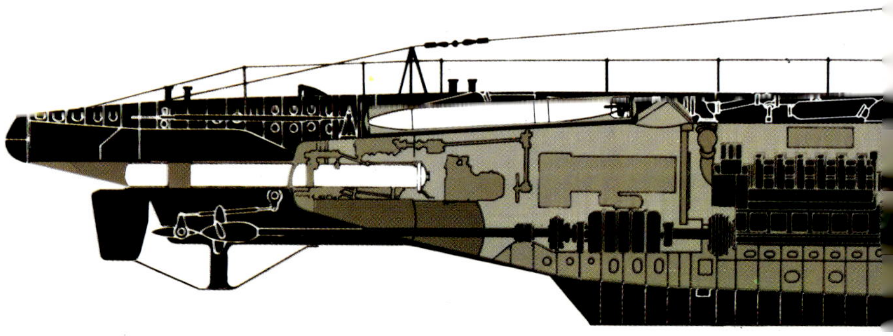

Above left: British submarines alongside their tender. Above: U-boat crewmen on watch in the Atlantic.

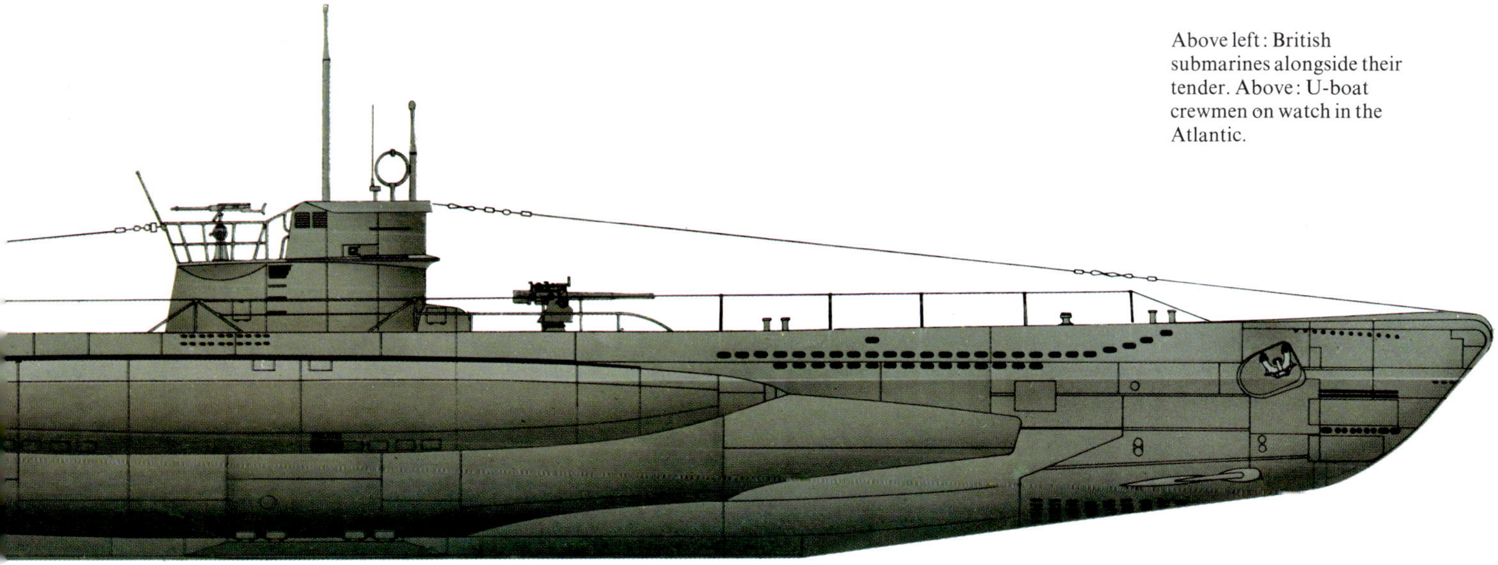

In these early days, the British attempts at offensive-defensive tactics played right into the U-boat commanders' hands. Escorts tended to charge off in pursuit of a contact or reported periscope sighting and spend far too much time on these wild-goose chases before rejoining their charges. Meanwhile the U-boats worked in close to the convoy and set about their work, virtually uninterrupted. It was at this time that 'Silent Otto' Kretschmer of *U-99* perfected his technique of working his way *inside* the convoy, between the columns of merchantmen. He went on to become the top-scoring U-boat ace of World War II, with a total of 44 merchantmen (266,629 tons) and one destroyer sunk. He and his comrades certainly had all the scope they needed. In the case of SC-7 the British only had two sloops and a single corvette with which to defend 30 merchant ships taking up five square miles of ocean.

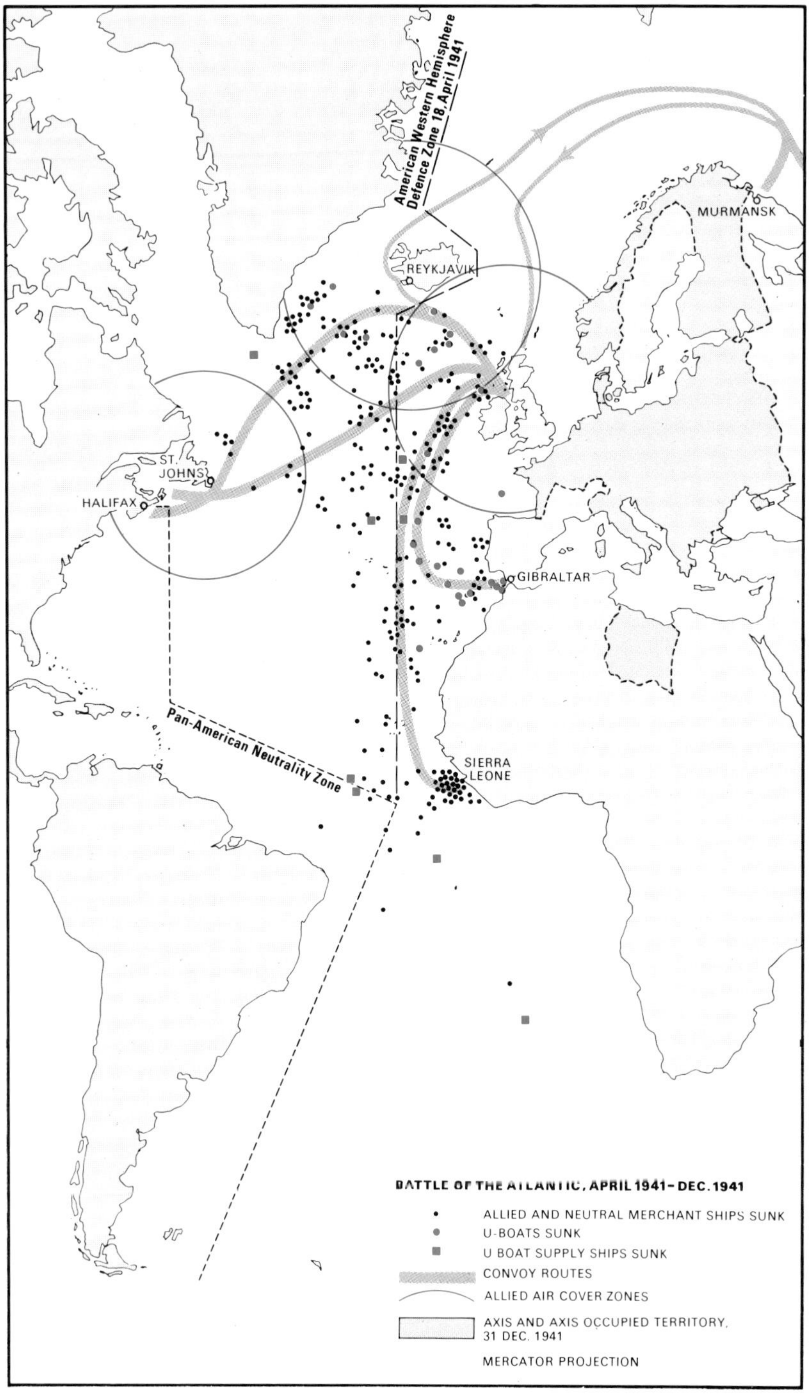

The following table shows the peaks of success reached by the U-boats during the Battle of the Atlantic after their devastating beginning in October 1940:

Month/ Year	*Merchant ships sunk (tons)*	*U-boats operational*	*U-boats sunk*
October 1940	63 (352,407)	27	1
June 1941	61 (310,143)	65	4
June 1942	124 (623,545)	140	3
March 1943	82 (476,349)	240	15

From a strategic viewpoint the Battle fell into three phases. The first (August 1940–December 1941) saw the U-boats easily take the strain as the Royal Navy's escort famine began to ease at last, and as escort commanders began to apply more successful tactics. The second phase (December 1941–June 1942) saw the entry into the war of the United States (a country almost totally unprepared for undersea war) bring little or no immediate easement on the Atlantic convoy routes. This was the second 'happy time', as the U-boats again went for the easy meat—this time along the American seaboard. The third phase (June 1942–May 1943) saw the U-boats, now over five times more numerous than in October 1940, going all-out for the domination of the North Atlantic—only to fail spectacularly, with unprecedented loss. And their failure lay in the growing inability of the U-boats to wage commerce warfare against a formidable combination of new technology, new weaponry and new tactics painfully developed over the past three years.

By the spring of 1941 the most urgent requirement of the British—more escorts—was being fulfilled as the stop-gap vessels ordered in 1939 and 1940 continued to be rushed into service. Their original requirement was simple: to be able to operate in the North Atlantic, carrying sonar and depth-charges. But from March 1941

they began to carry additional equipment which, when tested and proven, added significantly to their effectiveness. First came the newly developed 10cm Type 271 radar, whose narrow beam could locate a U-boat's conning tower (and, given ideal conditions, a periscope) even on a pitch-dark night. Then came High Frequency Direction Finding—HF/DF or 'Huff-Duff', which latched on to U-boat radio messages and enabled a U-boat's position to be plotted with lightning speed, no matter how short the intercepted message might be. Like Type 271 radar, 'Huff-Duff' was a standard fitting in new escort vessels by the end of 1941.

The invaluable British lead in radar development provided the next important weapon for fighting the U-boats: ASV (Air/Surface Vessel) radar, suitable for fitting in long-range shore-based patrol aircraft. As its name implies it could locate surfaced submarines as well as ordinary ships, but its weakness was that the radar contact tended to fade at short range as the aircraft came in at low level to attack. The answer to this particular problem was the 'Leigh Light', an intensely bright narrow-beam searchlight carried by the aircraft, used to illuminate the target once the ASV radar indicated that the target should be within visual range. By the summer of 1942 ASV radar and the Leigh Light were making surface runs in the Bay of Biscay suicidal for U-boats leaving or returning to port. The U-boat, roaring along on its diesels, would suddenly be dazzled by the Leigh Light's beam after the attacking aircraft had followed up an ASV contact with a stealthy approach. This the Germans countered, for a time successfully (July 1942–March 1943), with the Metox radar detector, known as the 'Biscay Cross' from its simple cruciform aerial. Metox told the U-boat when it was under radar surveillance and provided an eight-month respite from ASV and Leigh Light detection until the crucial month of March 1943, when the first successful contact was made with 10cm ASV which Metox could not detect.

Unless the U-boat was damaged or determined to fight it out on the surface, an aircraft pouncing on a surfaced U-boat normally only had a matter of seconds in which to attack before the U-boat dived. Once the U-boat was down it could change course sharply and make off while the aircraft depth-charged the area where the U-boat had last been seen. Once air-to-surface engagements became commonplace the British were able to analyse the problem and see that normal depth-charge settings were no use; the U-boat had no time to get down to the depth at which the charges were set to detonate. The answer to this was a new choice of shallow-depth settings from as little as 25 feet, which

Above: This U-boat is either unable to dive or has chosen to fight it out on the surface. Her diesels are clearly still delivering full power but the attacking Sunderland's last pattern of depth charges has straddled her amidships, ensuring her doom. Left: The deadly eye—Leigh Light on a Sunderland, for pinpointing surfaced U-boats at night.

Far left: Building U-boat pens, bomb-proof until the RAF adopted the devastating 'Tallboy' bomb. Left: U-boats in mass production. Right: A U-boat's ensign, the Reich 'War Banner'. Far right: A tanker burns. Below: British destroyer men hungrily await the results of a depth-charge attack.

Opposite: Aerial view of an escort's attack, with an encouraging oil slick welling from the turmoil of her last depth-charge. Opposite below: Depth-charge on its thrower. Right: 'Hedgehog' grenades mounted for firing (below) and (top) hitting the water.

caught the U-boat when it was still close to the surface and pushed up the rate of sinkings by air attack fourfold.

To make certain of a U-boat, however, surface escorts had to try and pass directly overhead, 'running down' the sonar contact until the accelerating echo return formed an uninterrupted tone. Against an experienced U-boat commander, wise in judging escorts' behaviour by hydrophone, this was hard to achieve. Escort commanders clamoured for a weapon which could be hurled ahead of an escort running down a contact. The result was the 'Hedgehog' projector which threw 24 small bombs, fused to explode on contact, over a a range of 250 yards. 'Hedgehog's' great advantage was that it gave the U-boat on the receiving end no advance warning to take evasive action, which conventional depth-charge attacks did. 'Hedgehog' came into service early in 1943, in time for the crisis of the Atlantic battle. Other unwelcome surprises for

the U-boats at this time were the new deep setting of 500 feet for depth-charges and the technique of enabling escorts to fire much denser patterns of ten charges. These, like 'Hedgehog' exploited the scatter effect and increased the chances of a hit.

Tactics improved rapidly after the establishment of a tactical evaluation and training school by Captain Gilbert Roberts in January 1942—the first time that the hard-won experience of

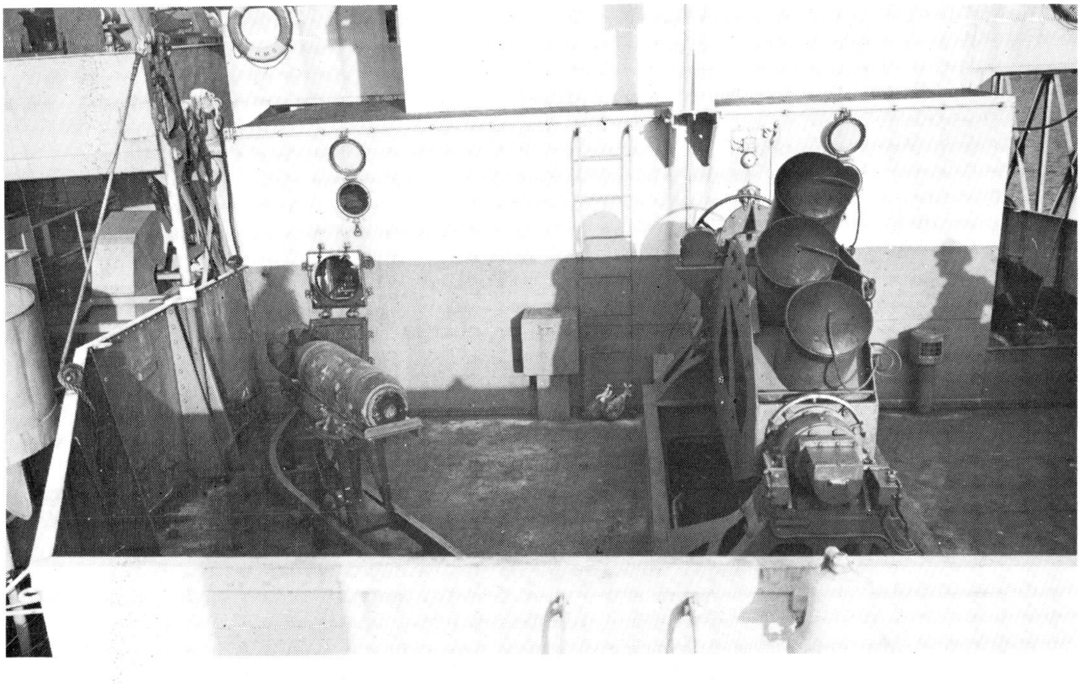

'Squid' forward-throwing mortar fitted in a British corvette in the latter months of World War II.

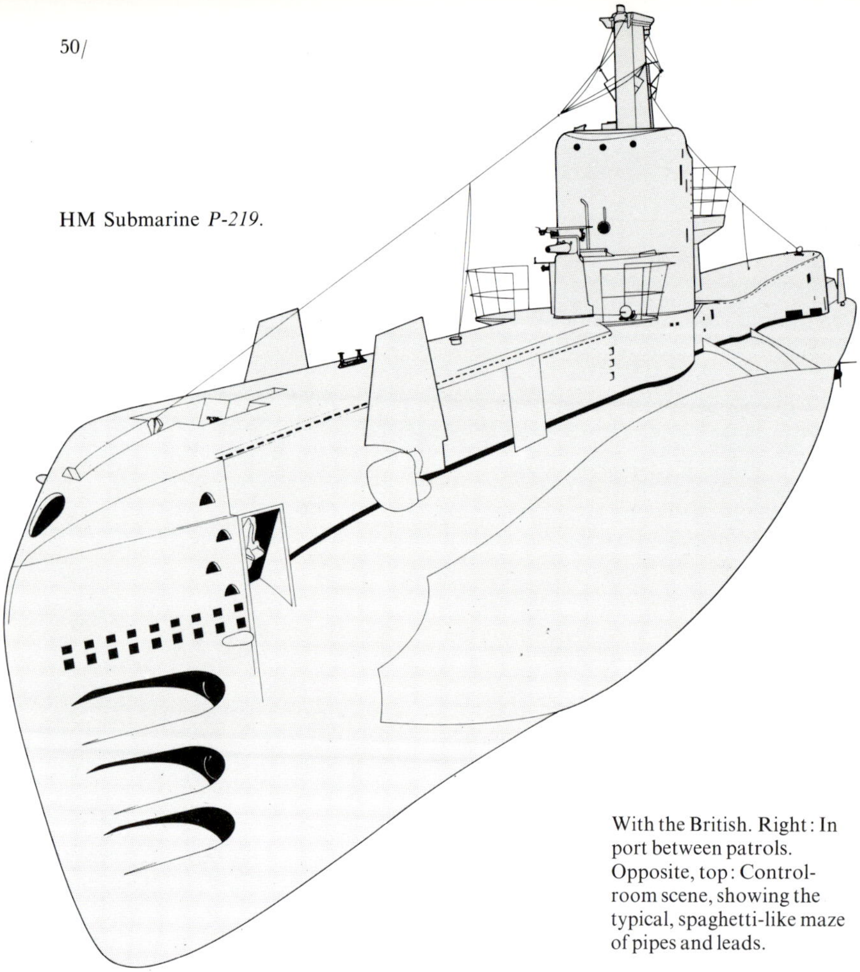

HM Submarine *P-219*.

With the British. Right: In port between patrols. Opposite, top: Control-room scene, showing the typical, spaghetti-like maze of pipes and leads.

The British take charge of a new 'fish'.

The British engine-room crew amid the roar of the diesels.

escort commanders was used to established how the U-boats were operating, and how best the escorts could collaborate in defence. In this collaboration a great boon was the American radio telephone, the TBS or 'talk between ships', cutting out the laborious signalling which did so much to slow down the escorts' reactions. With TBS and the new weaponry, the special escort groups, commanded by such veteran U-boat killers as Captain John Walker, Commander Peter Gretton and Captain Donald Macintyre, struck back with devastating effect in April and May 1943.

Even with all these new factors the final U-boat assault could hardly have been met without two other vital links in the Allied chain of survival. The first of these was the immense swelling of Allied merchant tonnage replacement by the American shipbuilding industry—a life-saving transfusion which, in early 1943, outstripped the losses to U-boats for the first time since autumn 1940. In July 1943, for the first time in the war, new tonnage overtook losses from *all* causes—submarines, mines, air and surface attack, collisions, weather and unknown causes combined. And the final link was the timely provision of long-range air cover over the 'Black Gap' in mid-Atlantic—the killing-ground, so long out of reach of shore-based aircraft, where the U-boats concentrated their last assault on the Allied Atlantic lifeline. The key air weapons were land-based B-24 Liberator bombers, and lightweight escort carriers to accompany the convoys. For the past six months the escort carriers and support groups had been drawn away from the Atlantic to cover the convoys first carrying, then supplying the Allied invasion of northwest Africa—Operation Torch. When the escort carriers and support groups were released and rushed back to the North Atlantic at the end of March 1943, they came in the nick of time. Out of a total of 240 operational U-boats, Dönitz had committed no less than 112 to severing the Atlantic convoy route.

Such an unprecedented concentration—which was only ever reached in the North Atlantic—

The blazing grave of a tanker.

The prefabricated, mass-produced 'Liberty Ship', potent weapon in the Atlantic battle. Top: A typical cargo. Above: Hoisting aboard a pre-fabricated deckhouse section. Right: Liberty Ships in varying stages of completion at the Kaiser yards in 1943. The ship in the centre is about to be launched.

proved capable of overwhelming conventional escort forces lacking hunter-killer support groups, long-range air patrols and escort carriers. Before these returned to the North Atlantic at the end of March 1943, the escorts of convoys SC-122 and HX-229 were swamped by a concentration of 38 U-boats as the two convoys struggled across the 'Black Gap' (15–19 March). Out of 92 ships, 21 (141,000 tons) were sunk for the loss of only one U-boat. But the passage of ONS-5 (22 April–6 May) was a very different story. Thirty U-boats were concentrated against this convoy of 40 (the latter considerably disrupted by atrocious weather) and managed to sink 21 merchant ships—but it cost them no less than seven U-boats.

With one U-boat being sunk for every three merchant ships, small wonder that the still-dense U-boat packs showed increasing reluctance to press home attacks on succeeding convoys, though well-placed to do so. In the decisive convoy battles of May a staggering total of 41 U-boats was sunk: 14 by surface escorts, 11 by air escorts, the rest on passage. Losses on this scale threatened nothing but the early annihilation of the entire U-boat force. In 1942 87 U-boats had been sunk, an average of 7.25 per month, bringing the overall total of boats sunk since the outbreak of war to 153, or an average of 3.8 per month. But 96 U-boats were sunk in the period January–May 1943, pushing the average monthly losses up to 19.2 for that year and to

U-boat under attack from American carrier-based aircraft, summer 1943.

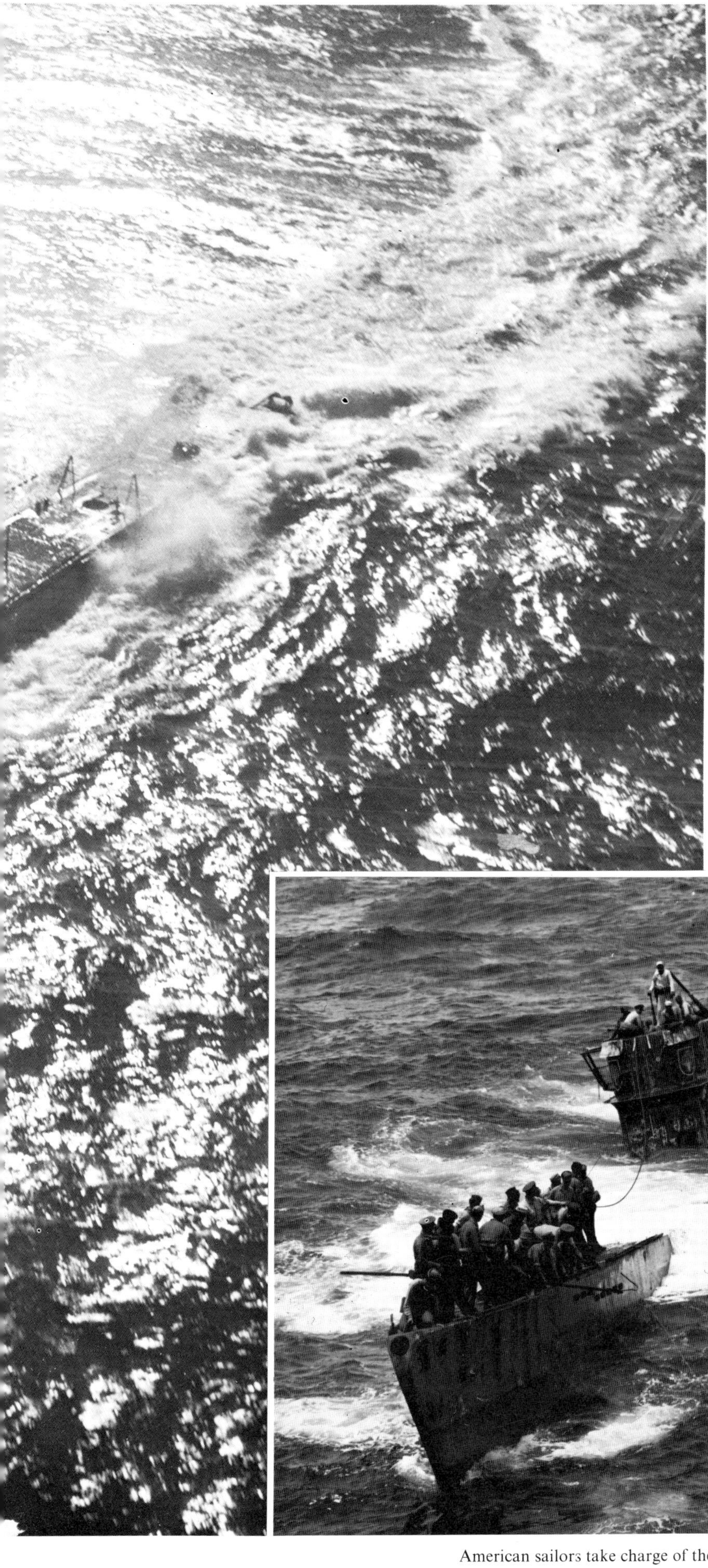

5.5 since the outbreak of war. Accepting the inevitable, Dönitz ordered his U-boats to withdraw from the North Atlantic routes on 24 May 1943.

The defeat of the U-boats in May 1943 was the defeat of the diesel-electric submarine by a combination which the Allies only managed to bring together at the last possible moment—carrier-based and long-range shore-based air cover, plus hunter-killer escort groups, HF/DF, 10cm radar and improved anti-submarine weapons and tactics. If Dönitz had had his 240 operational boats as late as 1942, long before all these improvements had been made to the defences and the transformed Allied shipbuilding programme had got under way, the Atlantic convoy route would most definitely have been severed and Britain probably starved into surrender by the end of the year.

But one of the main reasons for Germany losing World War II was the built-in opportunism of German grand strategy, with the resultant failure to concentrate on the Allies' weakest points. Dönitz's pleas to be allowed to concentrate his efforts in the North Atlantic were overruled after Rommel's first offensive opened a promising new front in North Africa (March–April 1941). Dönitz was subsequently ordered to divert U-boats to the Mediterranean, and

American sailors take charge of their prey. *U-505*, surrendered off the Cape Verdes in June 1944.

also to the Far North to operate against the Allied convoys to Russia. The resultant dispersal of effort, which saw a grand total of 62 U-boats written off in the Mediterranean alone by the end of the war, was of vital importance to the Battle of the Atlantic. By the spring of 1942, far from preparing for a knock-out blow against the North Atlantic convoy route, the U-boat force was being diluted into no less than three sideshows: the Mediterranean, the Far North, and the easy killings off the American coast. This strategic blunder, for which Hitler and Grand-Admiral Raeder must share the blame, gave the Allies just enough margin in the North Atlantic on which to survive in 1942.

In the Mediterranean, British submarine operations against the Axis convoys carrying supplies to the German and Italian Armies in Africa were no less deadly than the efforts of the U-boats in the Atlantic, though on a smaller scale. The British attacks on the Axis Libyan convoy route were supplemented by air strikes from Malta, and the submarine flotilla based on the island gave the British submarine service its most famous aces of the war: Malcolm Wanklyn of *Upholder*, 'Tommo' Tomkinson of *Urge*, Alistair Mars of *Unbroken* and Ben Bryant of *Safari*. This 'front' of the undersea war was not, as in the North Atlantic, a matter of group attacks directed from a shore-based headquarters, but of individual flair on patrol. British submarine commanders were considerably helped by the Germans' and Italians' lack of the sophisticated detection equipment used against the U-boats in the Atlantic. They also had plenty of scope for the ideal use of the diesel-electric submarine, perfected by Lothar de la Perière and *U-35* in World War I: surface attack with the gun. During the air siege of Malta (January–May 1942) the submarines performed invaluable service as supply ships, a role to which they were hardly suited. Though forced to quit Malta for three months during the massive German air raids of April–early May 1942, the submarines returned in July, after Rommel had been finally halted at Alamein. From then on, again working in harness with the air strike forces, the Malta submarines kept Rommel starved of fuel and reinforcements until Montgomery attacked with crushing superiority in late October.

The negligible contribution of Italy's submarines to the undersea war was one of the most welcome surprises to the British. Italy came into the war in June 1940 with 100 submarines, double the German strength, but soon proved that mere numbers were of little use without aggressive and skilled commanders working to a prearranged tactical programme. Italy's submarines achieved nothing of any significance, either in commerce destruction or in operations against Allied warships. The 26 Italian submarines operating in the Atlantic by the end of 1940 failed ignominiously to share in the 'happy time' then being experienced by their German allies. In 1940 and 1941 the complete inability of the Italian submarines to impede, let alone cripple the British Mediterranean Fleet was a key motive for the diversion of German U-boats from the Atlantic to the Mediterranean. All the severe British naval losses to submarines in the

Mediterranean—the battleship *Barham*, aircraft-carriers *Eagle* and *Ark Royal*, the cruiser *Galatea*—were inflicted by German U-boats. By the time of the Italian surrender in September 1943, 86 Italian submarines had been sunk or captured—18 of them by British submarines—double the number of German U-boats sunk by Allied submarines since the outbreak of war.

By the second half of 1943 Dönitz and the U-boat designers were struggling to find an answer to the new air/sea superiority of the Allied escort forces. The German efforts to beat the escorts led to a host of experimental fittings, modifications, techniques and tactics. Some of these were fundamentally mistaken; others became essentials of postwar submarine design. Dönitz's initial order for U-boats to 'fight it out' with aircraft on the surface was a disastrous miscalculation; only a handful of Allied aircraft was actually shot down, and aircraft were always easier to replace than U-boats. Even when the latter were given 37mm and quadruple

Above: The shattering end of the British battleship *Barham*. Below: The last hours of *Ark Royal*, which went down as rescuers struggled to tow her into Gibraltar.

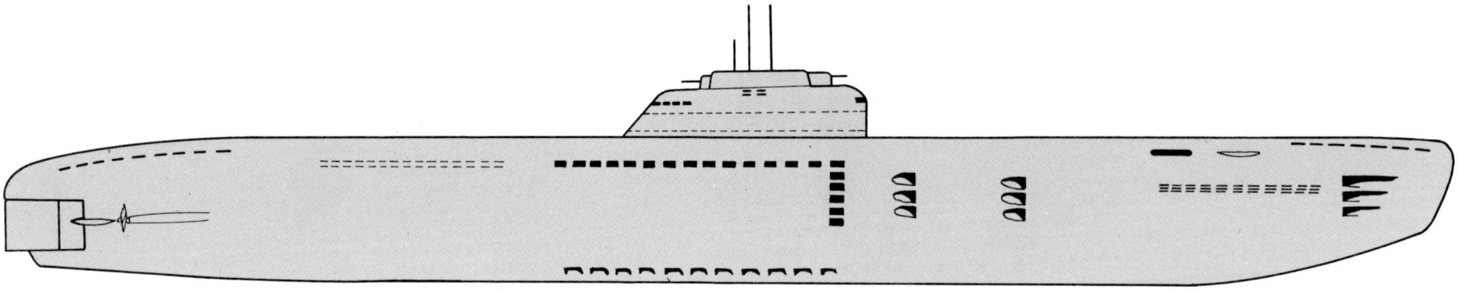

Top: Type XXI U-boat. Above: Unfinished Type XXIs pack the slipways at Hamburg. Thanks to prefabrication and the dispersal of manufacture, Dönitz's fleet of Type XXIs was fast nearing completion by the spring of 1945.

20mm AA guns the odds remained in the attackers' favour, and between June and December 1943 95 U-boats were sunk by aircraft alone.

Against the surface escorts the Germans adopted the *Zaunkönig* acoustic torpedo, which homed on high-speed engine noises. Though this primitive homing torpedo obliged Allied escorts to stream noise-emitting 'Foxers' it could not, once the mass attacks on the convoys had been suspended, reverse the course of the Atlantic battle by itself. Less successful was the *bold* or *pillenwerfer*, akin to the decoy cloud of ink emitted by a panicked octopus or squid. The *bold* was a slug of chemicals which, on ejection from the U-boat, foamed into a dense cloud of bubbles capable of returning a sonar echo. Trained sonar operators, however, soon learned to tell the difference. Nor could either the sharp ear of sonar nor radar be foiled by the expedient of covering U-boats with absorbent rubber (*sumpf*). But when the Germans turned to the *schnorkel* as yet another possible answer to their troubles in the undersea war, they opened a radical new chapter in the history of submarine development.

The *schnorkel* was not originally a German device; it was developed before the war by the Dutch, and fell into German hands when Holland capitulated in 1940. It enabled a submarine to run on diesels, either trimmed down or at periscope depth, with only a small air-breathing and exhaust head showing above the surface. Originally a device for stretching the life of a submarine's battery, the *schnorkel* offered the Germans a chance of preventing their U-boats being detected by radar and Leigh Light while recharging their batteries on the surface. Small though it was, a *schnorkel* head was not 'radar-proof', but when fitted with a radar detection device it gave prompt notice of Allied surveillance. And though a '*schnorkelling*' U-boat had to keep its speed down to about six knots it had a vastly improved range over a boat forced to rely on its electric engine for maybe 20 hours out of the 24. When there was enough surface wind to dispel the cloud of exhaust smoke, a *schnorkel* was hard to spot from the air. It was easily confused with breaking waves, 'willywaws' or miniature waterspouts travelling along the surface, and even spouting whales. In the last nine months of the war Coastal Command aircraft 'sighted' 216 *schnorkels* in British home waters, only 88 of which (from the number of U-boats actually at sea) can have been genuine sightings.

To the old U-boats with which Dönitz had fought and lost the first round of the Battle of the Atlantic, the *schnorkel* was of little practical use as a potential war-winner. But when fitted to the new, high-speed boats rushed through production in the last 18 months of the war it created an entirely new weapons-system: the fast, long-range *true submarine*, as opposed to the *submersible* tied to the surface. The most revolutionary prototype was the Type XVIII, with its Walter turbine powered by 'Perhydrol': peroxide based, burned with oil, independent of outside ventilation and capable of delivering bursts of speed up to 25 knots. The biggest snag with the Walter turbine was the corrosive and highly explosive nature of the fuel—but this did not prevent a rushed development which only helped further clog the already congested U-boat production pipeline. Far more promising was the Type XXI. Here was the ocean-going diesel/electric submarine rendered capable of all-submerged operations, using an improved *schnorkel* and silent 'creeping' electric motors. Another 'first' for the Type XXI was mechanised loading for the torpedoes, cutting out the need for boats to retire after the first attack in order to reload tubes.

With type XXIs Dönitz planned to reopen the Atlantic battle in 1945, using aggressive new tactics. The Type XXIs would use their speed to evade hunter-killer groups during approach, then get right *under* the convoys and riddle the merchantmen with acoustic torpedoes. Luckily for the Allies, 'peace' intervened—but one Type XXI captain, *Korvettenkapitän* Schnee, made a dummy attack on a British force on the eve of the surrender. Schnee rejoiced at the ease with which he went clean through the destroyer screen without being detected, then closed to an easy firing position on the cruiser in the centre. He then retired—again without being detected. But this demonstration of the Type XXI's potential took place on 30 April 1945—the day Hitler shot himself. Had the Type XXIs and their coastal counterparts, the Type XXIIIs, been ready a year earlier, they would certainly have been able to disrupt the Allied build-up for the invasion of Europe. Like the *Luftwaffe*'s Me262 jet fighter, which came too late to reverse the course of the war in the air, the Type XXI had fallen victim to the retention of obsolete types which had outlived their tactical usefulness.

It is only in comparatively recent years that attention has been given to the no less decisive 'Battle of the Pacific', which was the Atlantic ordeal turned inside out. In the Atlantic the Allies were on the defensive, trying to save

Left: Crew of a Japanese *Koryu* five-man boat. Below: Japanese submarine *I-2*. Bottom: Japanese Type *RO-7*.

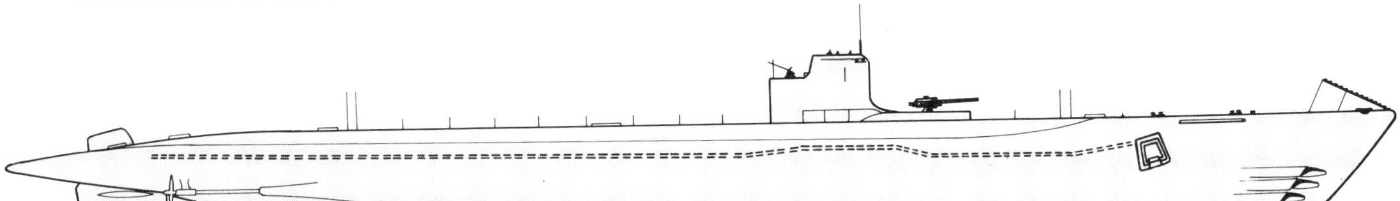

Left and below: The end of the US carrier *Yorktown* in the Battle of Midway, June 1942. Badly damaged by Japanese carrier aircraft (left), *Yorktown* was finished off by the Japanese submarine *I-168*.

their sealanes from the assault of the U-boats. In the Pacific, however, the Japanese, having conquered Southeast Asia, the East Indies, and the islands of the west Pacific by autumn 1942, suffered a similar assault from American submarines and failed completely to mount an effective defence.

As far as submarine strategy was concerned the Japanese had not advanced since the end of World War I, when the current obsession had been to make submarines work with the battle fleets. In the first year of the Pacific War, from Pearl Harbor to Guadalcanal, Japanese submarines did well enough in this role, their most prestigious 'kills' being the American carriers *Yorktown* and *Wasp*. But by the end of 1942 the runaway sequence of Japanese victories had been stopped for good, and the outcome of the Pacific War was being decided in the battle of attrition on Guadalcanal in the Solomon Islands. To hold Guadalcanal, and all their other widespread conquests, the Japanese should have concentrated on severing the vital Allied supply link between the American west coast and Australia. Their failure even to attempt this strategy enabled the Americans first to take Guadalcanal, then begin an advance up the Solomons chain in 1943.

Now the question was whether or not the Japanese Navy could defend the long sea routes connecting their far-flung island garrisons, and for this they were supremely ill-equipped. Their naval grand strategy was confined to

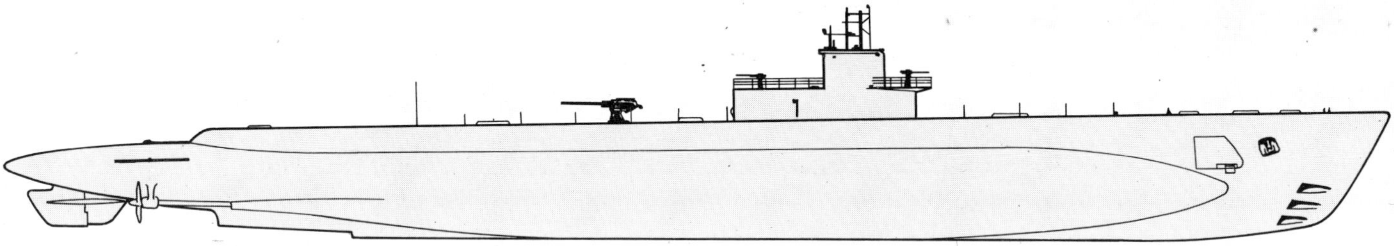

decisive operations with the 'Combined Fleet' of carrier strike forces and battle squadrons, and included no effective measures for the defence of the Japanese merchant navy. In December 1941, escort vessels ranked fifth in the Japanese naval building programme—a stark contrast to the top priority assigned to escort vessels in the British 1939 War Emergency, and 1940 Building Programmes. Moreover, the British had reintroduced convoy as soon as the war began—but the Japanese only adopted convoy in November 1943, having lost 22 warships and 296 merchantmen (total tonnage 1,335,240) in that year alone. At the same time the Japanese brought in an emergency escort-building programme—far too late to save their dwindling merchant fleet.

As for anti-submarine weaponry and technology, the threadbare and badly co-ordinated Japanese escort forces were pathetically ill-equipped. They relied on the depth-charge, supplemented by an Army trench mortar installed before the bridge. In the field of submarine detection, the Japanese Navy was still in the hydrophone era of World War I. About the only asset enjoyed by Japanese submarines was the excellent 'Long Lance' torpedo, one of the best weapons of the war. This travelled at 40 knots and was driven by liquid oxygen, leaving no track. But this was largely negated by the Japanese failure to use their submarines as an independent offensive arm. They never attempted pack tactics but tended to fritter away their submarine strength on lone gun bombardments of American atolls, or as communications ships, or as tankers for flying-boats. Another telling example of how Japanese submarine development had become stuck at 1918 was their persistence with aircraft-carrying submarines, long after the British and Germans had given up submarine monitors and cruisers. The Japanese 'I-400' class aircraft-carrying submarines were the biggest boats ever built

Top: American 'T' class submarine. Above: The last seconds of a diminutive Japanese freighter.

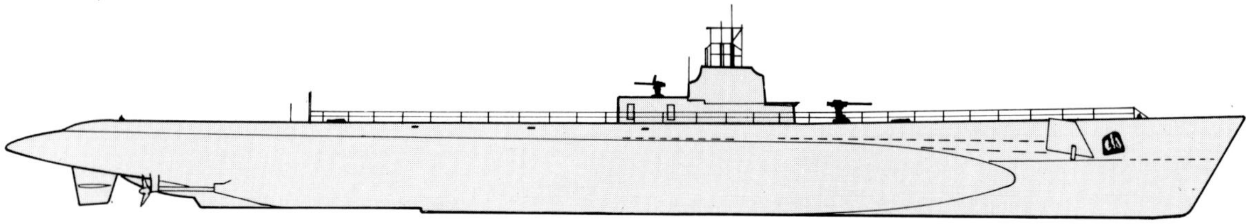

Left: American *Gato* class.
Below: Japanese 'I-400' class.

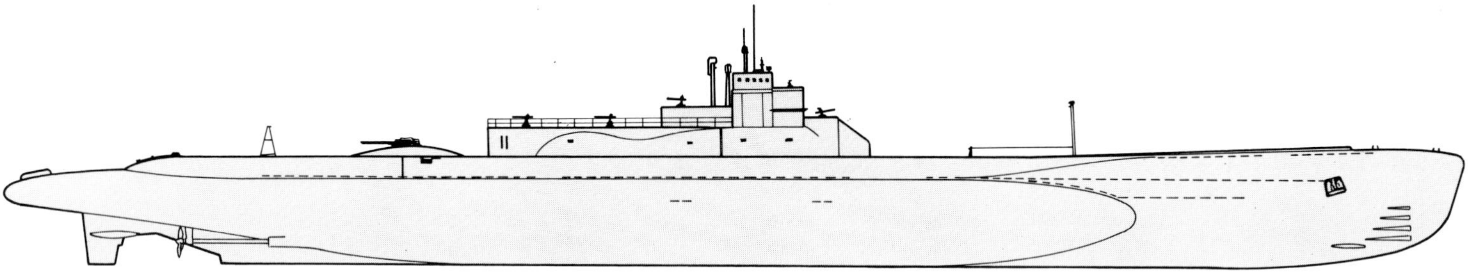

before the nuclear era; but there was little these 3530-ton behemoths could achieve and they had hardly more than curiosity value in the Pacific War.

The courage, dash and skill of the American submariners was backed by a firm strategic understanding of what submarines were for, and how they could best be deployed against the Japanese Empire. The American equivalent of Dönitz in the Southwest Pacific, Rear-Admiral James Fife, urged his submarine commanders to 'press home all attacks'. His standing orders continued: 'Pursue relentlessly, remembering that the mission is to destroy every possible enemy ship. Do not let cripples escape or leave them to sink—make sure that they do sink.'

An important American contribution to the development of commerce warfare was the use of submarine-borne radar to locate targets. The most prestigious kill inflicted on a radar-located target was made early on the morning of 29 November 1944 by Commander Enwright of the *Archerfish*, who fell in with the giant new carrier *Shinano* (64,800 tons) making her first shakedown sea cruise. After a six-hour chase Enwright fired a salvo of six torpedoes, all of which hit. Though it is only fair to point out that *Shinano*'s subsequent loss was due to inept handling on the part of her commander, she remains the heaviest warship ever to have been sunk by a submarine.

The campaign against the Japanese merchant fleet went from strength to strength in 1944. During that year American submarines accounted for 545 ships (2,140,000 tons). Tankers were the main prey at the beginning of the year and the record was held by Commander Dykes of *Jack*. On 19 February *Jack* encountered a small convoy of five tankers in the South China Sea and sank four of them in a running battle lasting all day. In April the US Pacific submarines were ordered to concentrate on Japanese destroyers. Hair-raising tactics were adopted to this end, such as the cold-blooded 'down the throat' shot—deliberately courting a ramming attack on the surface, and torpedoing the destroyer as it came in for the kill. No less demanding in skill was the 'up the kilt' shot: surfacing in the wake of a hunting destroyer and torpedoing it up the stern. The campaign against the Japanese destroyers was a resounding success: 39 of them had been sunk by submarines by the end of the war. The palm was won by Commander Dealey of *Harder* (lost with his

Opposite and below: Surrender of the giant, aircraft-carrying Japanese 'I-400' submarines in 1945.

With the Americans. Left: Captain at the periscope. Opposite, top: Diving officer and planesmen. Opposite, below: Crew quarters, forward torpedo-room. Below: Sinking Japanese merchantman, photographed through the periscope of USS *Aspro*.

ship in August 1944) who sank three destroyers in three days in June 1944.

The Americans took enthusiastically to group attacks, particularly after the Pacific submarine base was moved west from Pearl Harbor to Saipan in August 1944. American 'wolf-packs' were smaller than the German ones and were used more for target location rather than actual attack. As was the German practice, American 'wolf-packs' took the name of their senior officer, though with typical American flamboyance—'Blair's Blasters', and the like. But they had plenty to be flamboyant about. In June 1945 it was 'Hydeman's Hellcats' (nine boats led by Commander Hydeman in *Sea Dog*) who penetrated the inland Sea of Japan for the first time, carrying the sea war to Japan's doorstep by sinking 27 Japanese merchantmen

and the submarine *I-122* in 11 days.

By the time of the Japanese surrender in August 1945, the American submarine force in the Pacific had never risen above two percent of the massive naval forces deployed against Japan. But that two percent had sunk 240 Japanese warships and 2200 merchantmen—a grand total of 5½ million out of the six million tons of merchant shipping with which Japan had entered the war, and one out of every three Japanese warships sunk. The deadly work of the American submarines had made it impossible for Japan to supply, reinforce and defend every bastion of the immense sea empire which she had conquered in 1941–42. No other weapon-system made such a one-sided contribution to Allied victory in World War II.

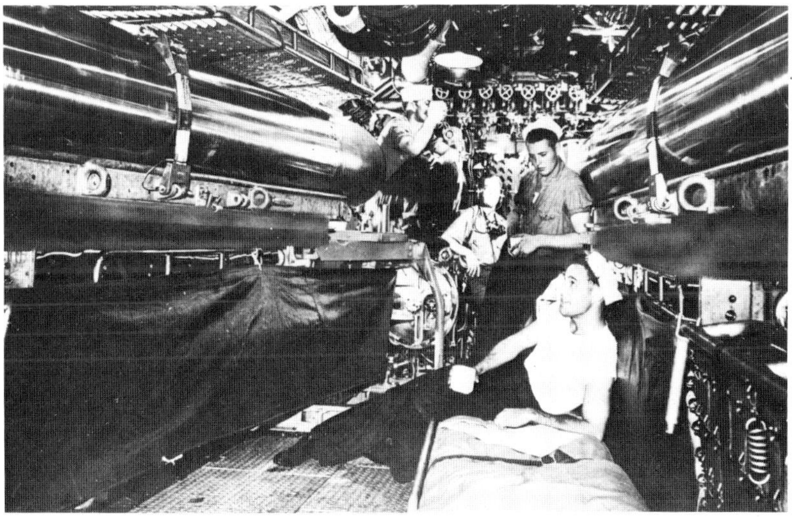

NUCLEAR GENESIS, 1944–1960

To the victor go the spoils; and for the Allies in 1945 the relative sophistication of Germany's last generation of World War II weaponry made those spoils rich indeed. The British overran Wilhelmshaven, Hamburg and Kiel, capturing not only the entire German naval archives but most of the technical information on the new U-boats. The Americans netted Wernher von Braun; other members of the German rocket programme were captured by the Russians. The advancing Russians had found leaner pickings in the captured German Baltic naval bases; but the Western Allies honoured their commitment to an even dispersal of all captured U-boats, an event which had the most profound effect on postwar submarine development.

A total of 156 operational U-boats had obeyed Dönitz's last order (4 May 1945) to surface, hoist the black flag and surrender. In addition to the U-boats which surrendered intact there were 221 others which had been defiantly scuttled by their crews; many of these could be salvaged. Finally there were scores of unfinished U-boat hulls and prefabricated U-boat sections still under construction at the moment of the German surrender, or abandoned because of bomb damage. Most of the latter were in the British sector. The basic share-out of intact U-boats was made on the basis of ten apiece to Britain, the United States and the Soviet Union; the rest were to be scrapped or sunk. In the New Year of 1946, 116 U-boats were sunk off Malin Head in Northern Ireland. Over the following year the Soviets tried to add to their quota by loading the unfinished German aircraft-carrier *Graf Zeppelin* with U-boat parts and equipment, but she hit a mine and sank while on tow to Leningrad in August 1947.

Apart from such refinements as automatic torpedo-loading gear, automatic depth-keeping gear (very necessary for taking the strain out of long runs at periscope depth), the *schnorkel* system, and radar-detection equipment, the biggest revelation was the source of high-speed power in the Type XXIs and Walter boats. The British had the luck to capture two operational prototypes of the Walter design (*U-1406* and *U-1407*). After handing over *U-1406* to the Americans they commissioned *U-1407* as HMS *Meteorite* and spent the next 12 years vainly trying to make Walter's explosive peroxide-based fuel into a safe operational proposition. As the Americans led the world with experience, money and resources for nuclear research they soon abandoned the Walter concept in favour of a nuclear power plant suitable for use in submarines. But all three of the navies which evaluated the Type XXI—British, American and Russian—wasted little time in adopting the Type XXI's best features to produce the next generation of diesel-electric submarines. And the spur for the latter development was the Berlin blockade, Russia's first detonation of an atomic bomb within four years of the Americans (1949) and the Korean War.

The basic receptacle of the Type XXI formula was a big streamlined hull carrying an electric battery double the size of those used to drive the electric motors of orthodox submarines. Increased hull size yielded a crop of further advantages: room to carry *two* or more electric engines, linked in tandem and room to carry more torpedoes and more electronic and automatic equipment were but two. Instead of phasing out their submarines of World War II vintage and courting the enormous cost of building new fleets of high-speed submarines, the Americans and British preferred the more economical alternative of converting their most modern types.

The Americans led the way with their GUPPY ('Greater Underwater Propulsive Power') programme, starting with 20 boats of the late wartime *Balao* class (improved *Gato*s with all-welded construction), and adding 15 boats of the *Tench* class. The boats were sliced in half through the engine room and a new 15-foot, 40-ton section was added amidships. The conversion was completed by a general cleaning-up: removal of the foredeck gun, and conversion of the traditional rounded conning-tower into a flattened, streamlined 'sail'. The Guppy conversions gleaned much valuable experience, yielding higher underwater speeds in the region of 15–17 knots, longer submerged voyages, and much greater manoeuvrability. They also proved able to dive to 600 feet. During the Korean War the *Tench* class Guppy *Pickerel* made an impressive run from Hong Kong to Pearl Harbor in 21 days without surfacing (1950). Two years later she demonstrated her manoeuvrability (not to mention the hardiness of her crew) by surfacing like a breaching whale from 150 feet at the spectacular angle of 48 degrees—one of the steepest surfacing angles ever attempted in cold blood.

The Americans quickly followed up their Guppy conversions with the six 'High Speed Attack' submarines of the *Tang* class, laid down in 1949–50 and all completed by the end of 1952. The *Tang*s pushed submerged speed up

524

to 18 knots, still slightly below their best surfaced speed. Performance breakthrough was achieved with the 'High Speed Test Submarine' *Albacore*, an unarmed prototype designed and built to test the fully streamlined 'teardrop' hull. Completed in December 1953, *Albacore*'s top surfaced speed was 25 knots, with a submerged speed of 33 knots.

Thanks to the lessons learned from *Albacore* the Americans were able to push the diesel-electric submarine to the limits of its potential with the three *Barbel* class High Speed Attack submarines laid down in 1956–57 and completed in 1958–59. These featured the teardrop hull pioneered with *Albacore*, a surface speed of 15 knots and a submerged speed of 25 knots.

The speed with which the Americans were able to develop these successive designs, each one leading smoothly to improved performances with the next, was due to the American genius for planning and creating the most suitable infrastructure for long-term projects. (It was to be demonstrated to perfection in the following decade, with the Mercury/Gemini/Apollo space programme.) The underlying confidence behind the method was in turn a direct legacy of the war years, when brilliant organisation had fulfilled President Roosevelt's declaration that the United States should be 'the great arsenal of democracy'. And it explained why as early as June 1952—only three months after the experimental *Albacore* had been laid down—work could begin on the world's first nuclear-powered submarine, the USS *Nautilus*, launched on 21 January 1954. On 17 January 1955 a historic signal was flashed from Long Island Sound: UNDERWAY ON NUCLEAR POWER.

As might be expected with such a revolutionary concept, *Nautilus* was a prudent, 'belt-and-braces' design with three engine-room levels, for propulsion by nuclear, diesel or electric power. Her pressurised, water-cooled reactor of enriched uranium drove two-shaft Westinghouse turbines, delivering a surface speed of 20 knots and a submerged speed of 23 knots. *Nautilus* was given a conventional, though highly streamlined hull, capable of diving to 700 feet. Though in every way an experimental type on which the entire future of submarine design rested, *Nautilus* was also built as an operational warship armed with six forward torpedo tubes. To guarantee her the longest possible service life, she was also given a Guppy-type hull to facilitate the installation of improved power plants.

The nuclear power plant was revolutionary enough in itself—the biggest milestone in warship propulsion since the Parsons turbine

Opposite: The launching of USS *Nautilus*, 21 January 1954. Above: *Nautilus* in Long Island Sound, January 1955—'Underway on nuclear power' Left: High Speed Attack submarine, USS *Tang*.

began to supplant the reciprocating engine in the early years of the century. But when married to the weapons system of the submarine it opened a completely new era in undersea warfare. Nuclear power cut the submarine completely free from the surface, ending the need for the air-breathing advertisement of the *schnorkel*. It gave the submarine unheard-of range (*Nautilus* steamed 69,138 miles on her original reactor core, which was replaced for the first time in 1957) and meant that the only limit on the time the submarine could remain submerged was the endurance of her crew. For conventional surface warships armed with conventional anti-submarine weapons, the implications of a submarine able to maintain speeds of over 20 knots at depths of over 500 feet were horrendous. They made the old depth-charges and mortar bombs of World War II seem like stone-age axes, and required new long-range sonar to detect this speeding menace in the depths. From her triumphant debut, less than ten years after American submarine designers had made their first examination of a Type XXI U-boat, *Nautilus* obliged every navy in the world to overhaul its anti-submarine defences and plan as best it could for a hazardous future.

The only serious setback to the new American nuclear submarine programme came with *Nautilus*'s successor, *Seawolf*, launched in July 1955. *Seawolf* was originally fitted with a liquid-sodium reactor instead of the pressurised-water type installed in *Nautilus*, but an ominous sequence of defects resulted in the removal of the original reactor and installation of a pressurised-water one. *Nautilus*, *Seawolf* and

Above: Successor to *Nautilus*—USS *Seawolf*.

their four successors—*Skate*, *Swordfish*, *Sargo* and *Snapdragon*, launched in 1957-58—established the 'first generation' of American nuclear submarines. They began to show the shape of things to come in 1958, when *Seawolf* shattered all previous records by remaining submerged for 60 days while making a 15,700-mile cruise in the Atlantic (6 August-6 October 1958). In the same year *Nautilus* made the first submerged crossing of the Arctic Ocean, crossing the North Pole on 3 August. A year later (17 March 1959), *Skate* found a 'polynya', or temporary open seam in the solid pack ice, and surfaced at the North Pole. After these voyages, strategy for future naval wars had to include the potential for operations beneath the Arctic ice.

The nuclear revolution was necessarily accompanied by a new departure in submarine navigation, for there was no point in being able to remain submerged for weeks at a time if the submarine still had to surface regularly to take

optical sights for navigation. The new system, first given its public demonstration on *Nautilus* and *Skate*, is known as SINS—'Ship's Inertial Navigation System'. SINS uses electronic and engineering precision to take the error out of dead-reckoning navigation. It takes the precisely-known geographical starting-point of every voyage as the basis for all subsequent calculations of position, constantly applying every alteration of course and speed. The accuracy of SINS permits a margin of error no greater than 200–300 metres after a circumnavigation of the globe—all completely free from outside detection, or of the need to surface for optical or radio fixes.

America's 'first generation' of nuclear submarines was rounded out by the six *Skipjack* class submarines, which were given the streamlined teardrop hull proven by *Albacore*. *Skipjack*, first of the class, was laid down in May 1956 and commissioned in April 1959; the other five had all been commissioned by the end of 1961. The *Skipjack*s broke the 30-knot barrier for submerged speed, but also served as a reminder of the prodigious cost involved in building a nuclear submarine fleet. *Nautilus*'s first reactor change had cost $20 million, but each of the *Skipjack*s cost $40 million to build.

The adoption of teardrop streamlining forced major rethinking in submarine armament, and hence in tactics. The pointed stern of the teardrop hull forced a concentration of the torpedo tubes in the bow; but the considerable increases in beam offered other possibilities. A World War II Type VII U-boat had a beam of about 16 feet; *Skipjack*'s beam was 31 feet. This gradual increase in beam led to the idea of mounting torpedo tubes laterally, able to fire to port and starboard instead of straight ahead. Such a facility would make possible a new breed of submarine: the 'submarine hunter-killer', or anti-submarine-submarine. Many times in the two World Wars, two enemy submarines had sighted each other on the surface or detected each other with hydrophones, and fallen into a tail-chasing circle. From its similarity to two dogs circling each other before coming to grips, British submariners had called this process 'doggy doggy'; it could only be broken by one submarine breaking off and escaping, or accidentally turning across the enemy's bow and stern tubes and exposing itself to torpedo attack. But a hunter-killer submarine armed with beam torpedoes would be ideally placed in such an encounter; and while *Skipjack* was still completing the Americans laid down the experimental *Tullibee*, commissioned in November 1960. She was the first submarine built with the bow position reserved for the active and passive sonar equipment needed for the detection and tracking of enemy submarines.

British postwar submarine development proceeded in a far lower key, without the political will, the money, or the nuclear research facilities enjoyed by the Americans. As the massive servicemen's vote indicated in the 1945 General Election, when Churchill was toppled from power, hopes for a brave new postwar world under a Labour government did not include restoring the Royal Navy as the world's strongest. Britain's economy had taken a terrible battering

Opposite: USS *Skipjack*, first nuclear submarine with the 'teardrop' hull pioneered by the experimental *Albacore*.

in World War II, which she had had to fight on credit. Britain was by far the biggest recipient of American financial foreign aid between 1945 and 1951, with a total of $6149 million in net grants and credits. (France came second, with $4328 million.) As the gradual conversion from Empire to Commonwealth proceeded through the 1950s and 1960s the Royal Navy retained a global role, but British submarine development came a poor second to maintaining the surface forces in the immediate postwar years.

The British long-term submarine programme after 1945 contented itself with applying the American Guppy technique to a selected number of wartime submarines. As the latter had always been smaller and slower than their American

contemporaries, it was hardly surprising that the performance of Britain's reconstructed submarines failed to reach the American level. The advantages of streamlining were frequently offset by the need to fit the cumbersome four-inch gun to submarines despatched to Commonwealth trouble spots.

Lack of funds for seaborne nuclear power research encouraged the British to continue tinkering with the Walter peroxide turbine system as a hopeful 'poor man's alternative' to nuclear power. As late as 1956–57 they were still prepared to lay down the experimental peroxide boats *Excalibur* and *Explorer*, the latter being known to her apprehensive crew as 'HMS *Exploder*'. The maximum performance claimed for *Excalibur* and *Explorer* was a precarious ten hours submerged at 27 knots, but the high consumption and dangerous instability of the fuel finally obliged the British to abandon the project in 1958.

By this date the first new British postwar submarines, the eight diesel-electric boats of the *Porpoise* class, were completing and the first of 13 *Oberons* had already been laid down. The best performance any of these boats could achieve was 12 knots surfaced and 17 knots submerged—a performance exceeded even by the American diesel-electric *Tangs* laid down some eight years before, and clearly inadequate for the nuclear era. Britain's decision to 'go nuclear' was made when the late Earl Mountbatten was First Sea Lord (1955–59). It was largely due to the relationship established by Mountbatten with Admiral Hyman Rickover, mastermind of the American nuclear submarine programme, that the British were allowed to purchase a complete nuclear power system for the first British nuclear submarine. This was HMS *Dreadnought*, a teardrop-hulled close

Opposite, top: 'HMS *Exploder*'—*Explorer*, Britain's experimental peroxide turbine submarine. Below left: HMS *Dreadnought*, Britain's first nuclear submarine. Below: *Dreadnought*'s captain at the periscope.

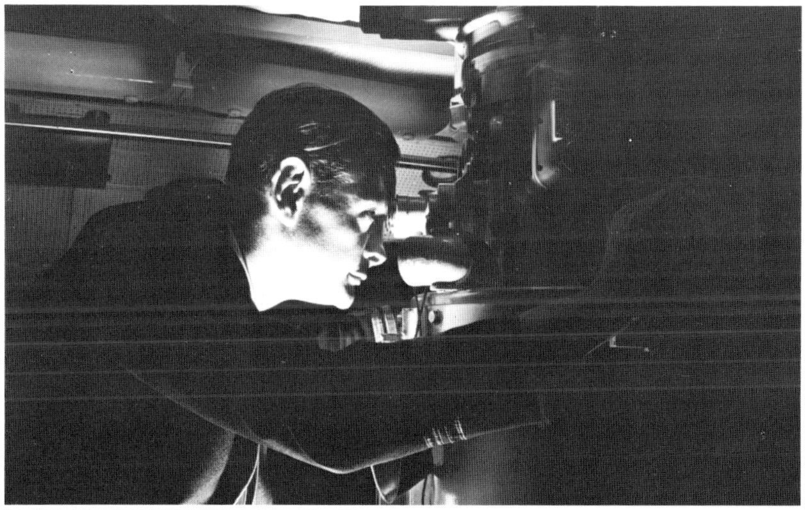

copy of *Skipjack*, laid down in 1959. When finally completed in the spring of 1963 she was given the peroxide-powered *Explorer* and *Excalibur* to use as high-speed underwater targets.

The Cold War began with Soviet land forces roughly matched in Europe, but with Soviet sea power derisory in comparison with that of Britain and the United States. This imbalance was clearly intolerable to the Soviet Union, obsessed with the security of its national territory after the terrible losses, human and material, of World War II. Stalin's decision to start building up a strong Soviet fleet was only to be expected, particularly after the formation of NATO (1949) and the awesome demonstra-

Below: British *Porpoise* class submarine, the first postwar diesel-electric design. Opposite: The long-serving *Oberons* gave the British taxpayer excellent value for money.

Soviet 'Whiskey Twin-Cylinder' submarine (the cylinders housing her missiles but making the type very 'noisy' when submerged), dressed overall for Soviet Navy Day in Sevastopol, August 1967.

tion of Anglo-American sea power in the Korean War.

Stalin's naval building programme of 1950–51 makes an interesting comparison with the German naval 'Z-plan' of 1938–39. Both aimed at the construction of balanced surface/submarine fleets, but whereas Grand-Admiral Raeder had envisaged a strong surface battleship/carrier fleet capable of achieving parity with that of the Royal Navy, the Soviet postwar programme headed by Admiral Kuznetsov accepted that the Soviet Union could never hope to match the carrier strength of the West. To counter the latter menace, Stalin approved the commencement of the biggest submarine-building programme ever envisaged—not as a commerce-destroying force, but as the only way of nullifying the range and hitting-power of the Western carrier strike forces. From the Russian viewpoint in 1950, the foremost naval object-lesson of World War II was not the commerce destruction achieved by the German U-boat force. It was, rather, the failure of the Japanese submarine force to stop the US Navy's carriers from ranging westward across the Pacific to the doorstep of Japan.

The programme envisaged building 78 submarines a year, starting in 1950, to produce a submarine force of 1200 boats by 1965. These would then hold a triple defence line across the sea approaches to the Soviet Union: 100 coastal boats for the innermost zone, 900 medium-range

marines was high. Above all it was overtaken by the scorching progress made with Soviet nuclear research, which enabled the first Soviet submarine reactor to be put in hand as early as 1953, and the first nuclear submarine to enter service within a year of America's *Nautilus*.

When the original programme was scrapped after Stalin's death, only about one-third of the projected submarines ever entered the water. These, the first Soviet submarines built after World War II, owed much to the German Type VIIs and Type XXIs taken into service by the Soviet Navy after the war: diesel-electric types with streamlined hulls, fitted with bow and stern torpedo tubes and *schnorkel*. About 240 of the medium type—the 'Whiskey' class, as it is known in Western nomenclature—were built between 1951 and 1957, and 25 'Zulus', the latter ocean-going submarines. The Russians originally hoped to power the 'Zulu' submarines with an improved model of the Walter turbine, but they had no better luck than the British with this power plant and eventually substituted the conventional diesel-electric system. The 'Whiskeys' and 'Zulus' were followed with impressive speed by the first Soviet nuclear submarine: the 'November' class, introduced in 1958. It was armed with bow and stern torpedo tubes and was reported as having a surface speed of 20 knots, a submerged speed of 25 knots, and a diving capacity of 1650 feet.

boats for the central zone and 200 long-range, ocean-going boats for the outer zone. This scheme contained a host of errors. It was an attempt to apply land strategy to the fluid problems of naval defence—a naval version of the zoned defences with which the Red Army had broken the last German summer offensive at Kursk in 1943, counterattacking to seize the initiative on the Eastern Front for good. It was a strategic misuse of the submarine, requiring an essentially offensive weapon to be used defensively. It was a dangerously restrictive programme because such a commitment took no account of the constant improvements being made to submarines at the time, and the danger of ending up with a vast fleet of obsolete sub-

Thirteen years after World War II, therefore, the submarine had virtually emerged as an entirely new weapon. Nuclear power enabled it to stay submerged on patrols of great duration, while inertial navigation guided it beneath the world's oceans, including the Arctic ice pack, with pinpoint accuracy. Now commerce destruction almost appeared as the least of roles for the most advanced submarines, like harnessing a racehorse to a farm cart. The future seemed to lie with the high-speed attack submarine, and with the hunter-killer seeking its prey in the depths. But those 13 years had also seen the American monopolies of nuclear weapons and nuclear submarines energetically broken by the Soviet Union. The nuclear arms race was on, and with it the search for the most effective—and unanswerable—delivery systems for nuclear weapons. As that search intensified in the late 1950s the submarine, with its capacious hull, was now pressed into service in its most awesome role: as the unseen vehicle for the 'ultimate deterrent'.

Attack submarine USS *Barb* at sea, December 1973.

The towering, streamlined 'sail' of USS *Finback*, *Sturgeon* class attack submarine.

Through the Arctic ice. Top: USS *Whale* surfaces at the North Pole, 6 April 1969. Above: USS *Trepang* breaks surface during exercise 'Wepex '71', January 1971.

THE DOOMSDAY SHIPS

Wartime pioneer of Polaris —test-firing of *pulver-raketen* from a submerged Type IX U-boat, summer 1942. *Right*: USS *Grayback*, designed to carry the Regulus cruise missile.

In military terms a country does not become a nuclear power just because it learns how to make a nuclear explosion. To guarantee full membership in what has been called the 'nuclear club', an 'independent delivery system'—independent, that is to say, of political control by another power—is essential. This delivery system can be of several types. The simplest of all is that used for small 'tactical' nuclear weapons for battlefield use: packing the nuclear device into the warhead of a shell and firing it out of a long-range gun. In 1945 Hiroshima and Nagasaki were destroyed by high-flying B29 bombers attacking in conventional style: flying directly over the target and dropping the bomb with parachutes, with a time fuse to explode it in the air over the target. But this had only proved possible because the Japanese no longer controlled their own air-space—they had no fighters capable of intercepting the B29s or anti-aircraft missiles capable of shooting them down. It was this danger that led to the adoption of remote-controlled missiles for the delivery of nuclear weapons, and the 1950s were the years of their begetting.

The latter years of World War II had seen a growing range of missiles used to deliver high-explosive warheads to their targets. After the war cryptic sets of initials, describing basic missile function, helped proliferate the nightmare jargon of modern warfare:

SAM—Surface-to-Air Missile
AAM—Air-to-Air Missile
ASM—Air-to-Surface Missile
SSM—Surface-to-Surface Missile

Nearly all the first missiles used in combat were short-range, solid-fuel missiles with no guidance systems, but by the end of the war the first guided missiles had been introduced. These were ASMs dropped from a parent aircraft and guided to their target by radio control, the latter being operated from the aircraft. This was the first system used to relieve bombers of the need actually to fly over the target in order to drop nuclear bombs—the 'stand-off' bomb, dropped from outside the enemy's AA gun and SAM defences and guided to the target under its own power.

In the early 1950s, however, the Americans and Soviets were pushing ahead with experiments in improving Germany's wartime 'V-weapons'. Two of these, totally different in type, had been used in the last year of the war, and both had proved capable of bombing London from the Continent. The first was the V1, a pilotless aircraft with stub wings—the first CM, or cruise missile. It flew on a pulse-jet engine and was just slow enough to be intercepted by the fastest piston-engined aircraft of the day, or shot down by barrage AA gunfire. But the V2 rocket, plunging down onto its target from its lofty flight trajectory through the stratosphere, was a totally different proposition. It could not be shot down or diverted in flight. It could be fired hundreds of miles from the target with no danger to a human crew. Here was the ideal vehicle for nuclear warheads, once sufficiently accurate guidance systems had been

Below: With the Polaris era only months away, USS *Halibut* test-fires a Regulus on 31 March 1960.

added to make sure of hitting the target, and sufficiently powerful rockets developed to make sure of reaching the target. This was the dreaded ICBM—Inter-Continental Ballistic Missile—which was added to the rival nuclear armouries in the late 1950s.

The trouble with the ICBM, however, was that it had to be fired from a 'fixed address'; it was too big to be moved around on mobile launching-platforms of the type used for the V2 at the end of the war. Once the ICBMs' launching site had been pinpointed by enemy reconnaissance it would naturally become the first target for the enemy's ICBMs. This led to two developments: the move towards 'second-level deterrence' (the ability to launch a second nuclear strike after the first one had brought down the enemy's retaliatory strike); and the frantic search for an effective Submarine-Launched Ballistic Missile (SLBM) which could be fired from any point within the enormous radius of a nuclear submarine.

As the Germans had found in the war, the cruise missile was the easier type to develop and by 1955 the American and Soviet Navies were both working on adapting the cruise missile for firing from submarines; it was referred to as the SLCM, or Sea-Launched Cruise Missile. The problems of the SLCM were twofold. First, the parent submarine had to approach dangerously close to the enemy's coastline; second, the missile had to be launched on the surface. The leading American cruise missile of the middle and late 1950s was the Regulus, and for a while continuing setbacks to the US long-range rocket programme brought Regulus to the fore as the only strategic nuclear missile capable of being launched from a submarine. In February 1956 the Americans announced that *Grayback* and *Growler*, originally laid down as diesel-electric attack submarines, were to be completed as guided-missile submarines for the deployment of Regulus. The two submarines were cut in two and cylindrical hangars installed above the bows to carry the missiles. Automatic loading and firing gear enabled the submarine to surface,

Opposite, top: One of the *Washington* class SSBNs—USS *Theodore Roosevelt*. Opposite far right: A Polaris A-3 missile breaks surface.

extract a Regulus from the hangar straight onto an inclined built-in launch ramp, fire the missile and submerge at once.

Grayback and *Growler* became operational in 1958 and within a year the Soviet Navy had countered with an equivalent stop-gap: the 'Whiskey Twin-Cylinder' conversion. Much clumsier than the built-in hangars used in *Grayback* and *Growler*, the 'Whiskey Twin-Cylinder' was, as its name suggests, a 'Whiskey' class boat with a couple of cylindrical missile hangars fitted aft of the sail. It gave the Soviets much-needed test experience with their new cruise missile, the SS-N-3 'Shaddock'. But it was, to quote *Jane's Fighting Ships*, 'Probably never truly operational, being a thoroughly messy conversion which must make a noise like a train if proceeding at any speed above dead slow when dived'.

For the American submarine fleet, however, the *Grayback* and *Growler* conversions proved to be no more than stop-gaps. After a traumatic three years in which it had seemed that the Soviet Union was well on the way to establishing a decisive lead over the United States in long-range rocketry, the Americans dramatically unveiled their Polaris programme and the giant new ships which would carry it.

By the second half of the 1950s the United States and the Soviet Union were working on the problem of launching the first orbiting satellite around the Earth. International prestige was the least of the prizes at stake. Orbiting satellites would transform global weather forecasting, electronic communications, and the gathering of astronomical data outside the murk of the Earth's atmosphere. They would also open a new era in both military and naval reconnaissance, surveillance, and as likely as not missile control and delivery from space. The result was a bizarre symbiosis between the nuclear arms race and space exploration: the techniques of mass destruction and the most inspiring challenge ever taken up by the human race paradoxically feeding off each other. And the powerful new rockets, improved control and communication needed to launch and recover spacecraft resulted in an ever-deadlier array of nuclear weaponry.

As the world knows, the Soviets were first into space, launching Sputnik 1 on 4 October 1957 and following it with Sputnik 2, carrying the dog, Laika, on 3 November. The immediate American reaction, from an understandable state of shock, was to risk and reap humiliating failure by unsuccessfully trying to launch the US Navy Vanguard satellite with maximum publicity. When Vanguard blew up on the launch pad on 6 December 1957, watched by a television audience of millions, credibility in the much-vaunted American technological superiority could hardly have received a more drastic shaking. Some of this credibility was restored on 31 January 1958 when the US Army's Explorer 1 satellite was launched, followed at last by Vanguard 1 on 17 March; but the Soviets countered on 15 May by launching Sputnik 3, weighing nearly 3000 pounds. The 31 pounds of Explorer and the three-pound Vanguard—scorned by Soviet Premier Nikita Krushchev as the 'Grapefruit'—caused deepening dismay when nuclear payloads were mentally substituted.

With the big Russian rockets grabbing the headlines in 1957–58, it was not easy to see how their supremacy had come about, or how temporary a phenomenon it was. The Americans had not rushed ahead with long-range rocket development after 1945 because they did not have to. They had the world's biggest strategic bombing force and carrier fleet already on hand for the long- and medium-range delivery of nuclear weapons. But Soviet rocket development, so triumphantly demonstrated with the first space shots, had been intended to cancel out and surpass American air supremacy. It enabled the Soviet Union to launch the first orbital satellites and manned spacecraft between 1957 and 1961—but this in turn prodded the Americans into developing their more sophisticated Atlas and Titan ICBMs for their Mercury and Gemini space programmes. By 1966 the United States had 904 ICBMs to the Soviet Union's 292.

With nuclear weapons as with the space programme, the Soviet rocket lead proved as superficial as it was temporary. The Russian obsession with developing heavy liquid-fuel rocket boosters for launching from land sites led to neglect of smaller solid-fuel rockets less suited to carrying the bulkier, cruder payloads created by Soviet technology. The Americans, on the other hand, while apparently completely outclassed by the feats of Soviet rocketry, were able to apply their superior technology and adopt solid-fuel missiles as a highly sophisticated nuclear delivery system. And these missiles, unlike the heavyweights with which Krushchev's USSR was making so much spectacular play, were sufficiently economical in size to be mounted in nuclear submarines.

The result was Polaris.

The Polaris formula took the streamlined, teardrop submarine hull of the *Skipjack* class—none of which had even been launched when Sputnik 1 went up—and stretched it by a breathtaking 130 feet, from 251 to 381 feet in overall length. The huge hull volume thus created was used to accommodate two rows of eight vertical rocket-launching tubes abaft the fin. Each of these 16 missiles could be assigned a different target and all were designed for underwater launching, the rocket engine cutting in as the missile broke surface and the guidance system correcting the missile's attitude to provide the correct flight trajectory to the target. And the real versatility of the Polaris formula was—and remains—immunity from retaliation by enemy land-based missiles, plus the unlimited initial radius provided by the submarine's nuclear power plant before a single missile is even fired.

The decision to introduce Polaris was taken while the United States was still being rocked by sputnik mania in the winter of 1957–58. Three new submarines specifically designed for carry carrying Polaris were ordered in the Supplemental New Construction Programme signed on 11 February 1958. Two more were ordered in July 1958. The lead ship of the class, *George Washington*, was launched on 9 June 1959 and commissioned on 15 November of that year. And on 20 July 1960, lying submerged off the Florida coast, she made the first successful firing of the new weapon. Two missiles were launched, their performance being carefully monitored from the nearby 'spaceport' on Cape Canaveral. The test was successful: the Polaris era had arrived. Two years later the Polaris system was given its first complete test, from underwater firing to warhead detonation. This happened on 6 May 1962 when *Ethan Allen*, first of the second batch of five Polaris submarines laid down between 1959 and 1961, fired a Polaris A-2 in the Pacific Test Area of Christmas Island.

With the Polaris concept, the role of the submarine as an instrument of undersea war changed completely. There were no precedents for this change, nor any convenient parallel case-histories of land, air or sea weaponry to make the change any easier to describe. The 'Strategic Ballistic Missile Submarine' or SSBN did not render all other types of nuclear and diesel-electric submarines obsolete. On the contrary, these continue to be built and introduced to service as a vital element of conventional naval deployment, supplementary to the posture of strategic deterrence. But the Polaris SSBN was the first warship deliberately designed to threaten the destruction of 16 enemy cities with their civilian populations. And the grim novelty of this role makes it impossible to consider the SSBN in the context of conventional undersea war.

When taken as an abstract, the SSBN is an object of despair to anyone inclined to disenchantment with the human condition. Here is the distillation of human knowledge and ingenuity in an ultra-sophisticated weapon of mass destruction. It is intended to help save the world from nuclear warfare by making its own use unthinkable, and yet its possible use as the result of human error or failure cannot be dismissed. Small wonder that objectors to the immorality and waste of nuclear weapons choose to focus their outrage on the SSBN as the deadliest and most insane menace of them all. And yet, given the destructive potential of nuclear weapons, it is still possible to look back over the first 20 years of the SSBN's existence and claim that it has not done badly as a deterrent. At the time of writing, we have managed to get through 35 years since the first puny atomic bombs were used on flesh and blood over Hiroshima and Nagasaki. During those 35 years, nuclear and thermonuclear weapons of far greater destructiveness have been contrived and brought to operational readiness—but none of them has been used, either by accident or design. The rulers of the superpowers have become adept in the art of crisis management in a crisis-ridden three and a half decades, which in a non-nuclear environment must surely have resulted in a Third World War. And 20 of those 35 years have been the years of the SSBN.

The advent of Polaris and its manifest advantages caused extensive restructuring of nuclear deterrent forces, both inside the United States and among her NATO allies. As more and more American SSBNs came into service through the 1960s and the stockpile of nuclear warheads grew, the former importance of strategic bombing forces began to recede. For example the total of American strategic bombers dropped from 630 in 1966 to 373 in 1977. After a costly flirtation with the American Skybolt stand-off bomb, Britain, in 1962, decided to wind down her strategic bombing force and adopt Polaris herself, building her own

With the French strategic nuclear fleet. Below: Testing the manual firing controls in the 'forest' of *Redoutable*'s launching-tubes. Below right: Loading an MSBS M-20 into one of the tubes. Opposite: France's SLBM, the MSBS M-1.

submarines but taking the American missile. The four ships of the *Resolution* class were laid down in 1964–65; *Resolution*, the first into service, was commissioned in October 1967. France followed suit with her *Redoutable* class, the first of which *Redoutable*, became operational in December 1971. Unlike Britain, France elected to develop her own missile 'family'. (Considerably advanced in rocket development over her European neighbours, the French joined the ranks of the space powers by putting their first satellite into orbit in November 1965, launched from a French-made Diamant rocket.) France went on to fit her SSBN fleet with her own ballistic missile, the MSBS.

In retrospect, one of the most intriguing points about the adoption of the SSBN is that it took place during the last 15 years of world affluence, 1958–73, before the Yom Kippur War in the Middle East and the ensuing world energy and economic crisis—for the financial cost was appalling. *Skipjack* had cost $40 million; *Ethan Allen* cost $105 million. As for the main American SSBN fleet of no less than 31 ships (*Lafayette* and *Benjamin Franklin* classes, laid down between January 1961 and March 1965) they cost about $109.5 million *each*. However, these were only the construction costs; on top of the amounts mentioned above one must add the cost of replacing nuclear cores (about $3.5 million apiece) and repeatedly up-dating the ballistic missiles as bigger and better models are developed. Quite apart from their SSBN programme, the Americans were proceeding with their huge nuclear-powered aircraft-carriers of the *Enterprise* and *Nimitz* classes, the biggest floating structures ever built. *Enterprise*, commissioned in 1961, cost $451.3 million; but the many delays to her successor, *Nimitz*, not commissioned until May 1975, increased its cost to $1.881 *billion*. And the combined defence appropriations for the American SSBN and nuclear carrier construction programmes were nothing to the $40 billion set aside for the Apollo

Opposite: British SSBN HMS *Revenge* at speed.

moon programme before the United States had succeeded in putting so much as a mouse into Earth orbit.

The decision of Britain to adopt Polaris deserves special comment. It was prompted by the obvious political conviction that the country should retain an independent nuclear deterrent. Given the fact that there were no conceivable circumstances under which Britain could find herself facing a nuclear conflict with the United States, and given the enormous destructive potential of the American SSBN fleet, it is highly questionable whether Britain's ability to keep two SSBNs constantly at sea (and she has not always managed to do even that) acts as a genuinely independent deterrent on the Soviet Union. Britain's increasing economic problems over the past 20 years, even with the safety-net of North Sea Oil, make the high cost of the British SSBN force seem an excessive price to pay for a nominally independent deterrent. (*Resolution* cost £40.24 million without her missiles, while the combined cost of *Repulse*, *Resolution* and *Revenge* was £116.05 million.)

Britain was, moreover, faced in the 1960s with a familiar menace which, after her traumatic experiences in the two World Wars, she should have been the first to diagnose. This was the rapid naval growth of a potentially hostile nation with submarine development in the forefront of its naval priorities. Between 1958 and 1968, the Soviet Union advanced from 21st to 5th place among the maritime nations of the world. In terms of economic vulnerability nothing has changed for Britain since World War II: her livelihood remains totally dependent on seaborne imports which have to be paid for with seaborne exports (in Britain's case with increasing lack of success). While nuclear devastation remains a nightmare possibility, starvation by sea inflicted by enemy submarines

Below: The Navigator at work in the control room of HMS *Repulse*.

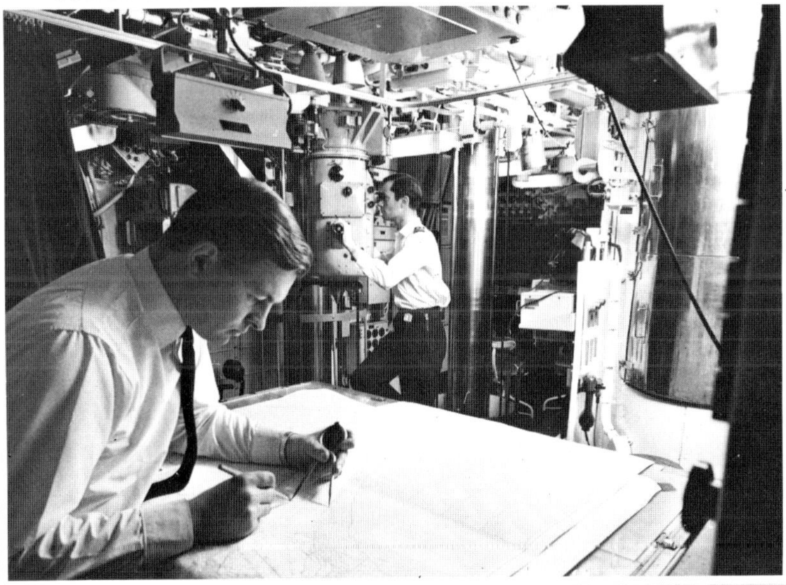

Left: USS *Whale* surfaced at the North Pole April 1969. Below: HMS *Resolution*'s galley. Bottom: A far cry from the cramped confines of the pioneering days—the helmsmen's positions in *Redoutable*. Right: The endless round of checks and tests. The Assistant Polaris Systems Officer-in-Charge at a monitoring panel in *Resolution*.

has twice provided a harrowing case-history in how Britain can be brought to the brink of defeat by conventional naval forces.

With the British Isles straddling the Soviet Union's naval exit-routes into the Atlantic, the money devoured by the SSBN force could have been spent to no less effect, and probably far better, on making it demonstrably impossible for Soviet submarines to operate in the North Atlantic without Britain's toleration. If Britain could hardly be expected to match the Americans ship for ship, building enough nuclear hunter-killer submarines to cope with a mass attack on the North Atlantic sealane by Russian submarines, she could certainly have built the strongest surface force in the Western alliance and contented herself with the main anti-submarine role.

Having elected to join the SSBN nuclear deterrers, however, Britain could certainly not afford to keep pace with the high-speed development of SLBM missiles. The original Polaris A-1 missile had a range of 1200 nautical miles. This was almost immediately improved by Polaris

Above: *Lafayette*, first of the US Navy's '3rd generation' Polaris submarines, is launched at Groton in 1962. Left: *Lafayette* class USS *Daniel Boone* at sea. Opposite, top: the 'forest' of launching-tubes in USS *John Adams*. Opposite, centre: Sonar watch in USS *Ulysses S. Grant*. Right: Commander of *Ulysses S. Grant* at the periscope, in a control room whose size and cleanliness few old-time submariners would have found credible. Far right: USS *James Madison* bids farewell to one of her Polaris tubes in 1969, scheduled for replacement with Poseidon.

A-2 with 1500 miles, and in October 1963 the *Andrew Jackson* fired the first Polaris A-3 off Cape Canaveral. Polaris A-3 not only had a vastly improved range of 2500 miles but it also delivered a cluster of three separate nuclear warheads to the same target. This 'parcelling' of nuclear warheads ushered in the second generation of submarine-launched ballistic missiles ponderously initialled as MIRV: 'Multiple Independently-targetable Re-entry Vehicle'. In the case of Poseidon, the first SLBM MIRVed missile and successor to Polaris A-3, this meant a missile which, like Polaris, can be carried by a SSBN and launched from under water with a range of 2500 miles. But once in flight its payload splits into ten mini-missiles, each capable of being steered to a separate target. Thus instead of being able to hit 16 enemy targets, as with Polaris, a SSBN armed with Poseidon can hit 160. The ten *George Washingtons* and *Ethan Allens* of the SSBN 'first generation' were not suitable for conversion to Poseidon, but by 1978 all 31 of the *Lafayettes* and *Benjamin Franklins* had been fitted with Poseidon. With

Polaris A-3 (left) compared with the larger, MIRVed Poseidon.

the Polaris missiles of the earlier SSBNs the overall American SSBN fleet was now able to fire a combined theoretical total (theoretical, because not all the ships are simultaneously at sea) of 5020 nuclear warheads—55 percent of the total United States nuclear deterrent.

But Poseidon was not to be the last word. In 1976 the Americans laid down the first of the giant (18,000 tons) *Ohio* class SSBNs. *Ohio*, first of the class, was launched in November 1978. She carries no less than 24 launching-tubes for

First successful launch of Trident, 8 June 1979.

the 'third-generation' SLBM, Trident, with MIRVed warhead and a nominal range of 4000 miles. *Michigan*, second of the class, approaches completion at the time of writing. It was hard to see the SSBN being evolved much further until, in mid-November 1980, the Soviet Union launched the first of her 'Typhoon' class giants. At 30,000 tons they are far bigger than many NATO aircraft-carriers, and though their 20 SS-N-18 SLBMs are believed not to be MIRVed they out-range Trident by 1200 miles.

Colossus—*Ohio* class Trident SSBN, USS *Michigan*, at Groton in April 1979.

First of the Trident giants: USS *Ohio* in the water, with the towering bulk of *Michigan* at left.

Caught completely on the wrong foot by the early American commitment to the SSBN, the Soviet Union spent a desperate decade of improvisation and experiment to develop an equivalent system. The first Russian method used for firing missiles from submarines (apart from cruise missiles employed in the long-range SSM role) consisted of lengthening the sail to produce a streamlined fairing capable of carrying ballistic missiles in two or three vertically mounted tubes. This process, begun as early as 1955 with converted 'Zulu' class boats, actually made the Soviet Union the first sea power to produce a ballistic missile submarine. But the

only Russian missile small enough to be carried in a submarine was the tiny 'Sark' with a range of no more than 300 miles, and by the late 1950s it was not to be expected that any diesel-electric submarine would be able to get within 300 miles of the American continent without being detected.

Nevertheless, this was the system with which the Russians proceeded into the 1960s, building small successive batches of submarines capable of carrying missiles of increasing range. The 'Golf' variants, 21 in all, were accompanied by the 13 'Hotel' class, appearing between 1958 and 1962; both were originally equipped with 'Sark', but subsequently equipped with the SS-N-5 'Serb', with a range of 700 miles. Experience thus gained led to the USSR's answer to the American Polaris SSBN: the 8500-ton 'Yankee' class, which appeared in 1967. The 'Yankee' SSBN imitated the whale-shaped, elongated hull of the American boats and also mounted its missiles in 16 vertical tubes—but the range of its SSN-6 'Sawfly' missiles was only 1300 miles, and even when improved in later marks this range still fell far short of the 2500 miles of Polaris A-3 and Poseidon.

The 1970s have seen the Soviet Union doggedly catching up with the enormous lead established by the American SSBN force in the 1960s. The 'Delta' class SS-N-18 missile took the Soviet SSBN force through the 5000-mile range barrier, and the first Soviet experiments with MIRVing were soon detected. In 1976, the first year in which comparisons in MIRVed warheads could be drawn, the Soviet Union was estimated to have only 140 missiles to the American 1046—or 2970 independently-targetable warheads (ICBMs and SLBMs combined) to the American 7274. By 1976 the Russians had produced the 'Delta III', armed with the SS-N-18 of no less than 5200 miles' range—capable of hitting any part of the northern hemisphere from Soviet-controlled waters. Soviet MIRVing continues to improve at the time of writing, and the likelihood of the Soviet Union achieving MIRV parity in the near future can be no more than delayed by the American Trident programme. The newest, 30,000-ton 'Typhoons' are also designed for the SS-N-18, but will almost certainly be used as test-beds for more sophisticated MIRVed Soviet SLBMs in the near future.

No class of warship other than the ballistic missile submarine has ever been able to unleash catastrophe upon the world—yet with each year that passes without nuclear war, the doomsday ships will continue to do their job. Lord Fisher's prophecy, back in 1904, of the 'immense impending revolution which the submarines will effect as offensive weapons of war', has been awesomely fulfilled. And it was also Fisher who had shocked the Hague Peace Conference of 1899 by asserting that 'War should be terrible! You may as well talk of civilizing Hell!' Like the great battleships which Fisher created, swinging idly round their anchors through nearly all of World War I, the merciful inactivity of the nuclear doomsday ships can hardly be considered a failure when the alternative is too horrible to contemplate.

Opposite, top: Soviet 'Zulu V' experimental boat: two ballistic missiles mounted in the sail of an otherwise conventional diesel-electric submarine, as spotted by air air reconnaissance in November 1970. Below: Soviet 'Yankee' class ballistic missile submarine, armed—like its American, British and French counterparts—with 16 launch tubes aft of the sail (August 1976).

576
576
342